M000087623

Readers Love Denise's Playful Math Books

"Reading one of Gaskins' books is like going to a really great teacher workshop—part philosophy, part practical ideas, and all excellent. She just oozes expertise and enthusiasm."

—Amy at Hope Is the Word blog

"It revolutionized our homeschool this year."

—Caitlin Fitzpatrick Curley, My-Little-Poppies.com

"It's a crime, really, that school makes math so boring, when there are so many ways to do the opposite, for anyone who wants to. Denise Gaskins's book is full of ideas."

—Sasha Alyson, online reader review

"With this approach I can teach my kids to think like mathematicians without worrying about leaving gaps ... I can't wait to take my children by the hand and head off to explore the wonderful world of maths."

—Lucinda Leo, NavigatingByJoy.com

A PLAYFUL MATH SINGLE

70+
Things To Do
WITH A
Hundred
Chart

NUMBER, SHAPE, AND LOGIC ACTIVITIES
FROM PRESCHOOL TO MIDDLE SCHOOL

Denise Gaskins

Tabletop Academy Press

© 2018 Denise Gaskins
Print version 1.01
All rights reserved.
Except for brief quotations in critical articles or reviews, the purchaser or reader may not modify, copy, distribute, transmit, display perform, reproduce, publish, license, create derivative works from, transfer or sell any information contained in this book without the express written permission of Denise Gaskins or Tabletop Academy Press.

Tabletop Academy Press, Blue Mound, IL, USA
tabletopacademy.net

ISBN: 978-1-892083-44-9
Library of Congress Control Number: 2018915121

DISCLAIMER: This book is provided for general educational purposes. While the author has used her best efforts in preparing this book, Tabletop Academy Press makes no representation with respect to the accuracy or completeness of the contents, or about the suitability of the information contained herein for any purpose. All content is provided "as is" without warranty of any kind.

CREDITS:

A huge "Thank you!" to my beta readers: Debbie, Judy, Olisia, Shaista, Susie, and Tara. Your comments improved the book so much.

Portions of this book were originally published on the Let's Play Math blog.
DeniseGaskins.com

Cover photo copyright © 2007 Thor (geishaboy500) via Flickr (CC BY 2.0).
flickr.com/photos/geishaboy500/570763679

"Find the Factors" puzzles by Iva Sallay. Used by permission.
findthefactors.com

"Ulam's Spiral at 41" image generated at the Alpertron website.
alpertron.com.ar/ulam.htm

"Play. Discuss. Notice. Wonder" photo courtesy of Steve Shreve on Unsplash.
unsplash.com/photos/olvffymayro

Author photo by Christina Vernon:
melliru.com

Contents

To begin developing thinking,
        you must first have a child who is curious.
For without curiosity, there is only forced thinking.

The problem with traditional math
        is it jumps to the punchline.
Absolutely no mystery or suspense
        is developed in traditional math books.

Why?

Apparently, someone thought
        math was without mystery.
That math is a definitive subject
        of rules and algorithms
                that all have been discovered.

We must persuade children
        that math is a worthy pursuit
through interesting stories,
        examining quirky math properties,
          and asking good questions.

—LACY COKER

It is paradoxical that many educators and parents still differentiate between a time for learning and a time for play without seeing the vital connection between them.

—LEO F. BUSCAGLIA

CHAPTER 1

Hundred Charts Build Number Sense

ARE YOU LOOKING FOR CREATIVE ways to help your children learn math? You don't need a special workbook, teacher's manual, or lesson plans.

All you need is an inquiring mind and something interesting to think about.

Play. Discuss. Notice. Wonder.

Enjoy.

In this book, we'll explore many ways you and your children can think about math with a hundred chart.

The hundred chart (also called a *hundred board* or *hundred grid*) is a ten-by-ten square array, usually drawn by hand or printed on paper. Ten rows, with ten squares in each row. One hundred squares in all.

Youngsters can play games on a hundred chart to build *number sense*, a feeling of familiarity and flexible confidence in working with numbers. Older students can explore multiplication and fraction concepts, which will give them a strong foundation for understanding algebra.

The squares in the chart may be blank or filled with the natural numbers 1–100, like a number line that has been cut and laid in rows. Some people prefer to use the whole numbers 0–99, which keeps the single-digit numbers and the numbers in each decade on the same row. Either style of numbered chart helps children master the relationships and patterns in our *decimal* (based on tens) counting system.

1	2	3	4	5	6	7	8	9	10
11	12	13	14	15	16	17	18	19	20
21	22	23	24	25	26	27	28	29	30
31	32	33	34	35	36	37	38	39	40
41	42	43	44	45	46	47	48	49	50
51	52	53	54	55	56	57	58	59	60
61	62	63	64	65	66	67	68	69	70
71	72	73	74	75	76	77	78	79	80
81	82	83	84	85	86	87	88	89	90
91	92	93	94	95	96	97	98	99	100

A traditional hundred chart counts down from the top of the page, like reading a book.

0	1	2	3	4	5	6	7	8	9
10	11	12	13	14	15	16	17	18	19
20	21	22	23	24	25	26	27	28	29
30	31	32	33	34	35	36	37	38	39
40	41	42	43	44	45	46	47	48	49
50	51	52	53	54	55	56	57	58	59
60	61	62	63	64	65	66	67	68	69
70	71	72	73	74	75	76	77	78	79
80	81	82	83	84	85	86	87	88	89
90	91	92	93	94	95	96	97	98	99

91	92	93	94	95	96	97	98	99	100
81	82	83	84	85	86	87	88	89	90
71	72	73	74	75	76	77	78	79	80
61	62	63	64	65	66	67	68	69	70
51	52	53	54	55	56	57	58	59	60
41	42	43	44	45	46	47	48	49	50
31	32	33	34	35	36	37	38	39	40
21	22	23	24	25	26	27	28	29	30
11	12	13	14	15	16	17	18	19	20
1	2	3	4	5	6	7	8	9	10

Many children find the bottoms-up hundred chart more logical than the traditional top-down version because it climbs up to reach the higher-value numbers.

90	91	92	93	94	95	96	97	98	99
80	81	82	83	84	85	86	87	88	89
70	71	72	73	74	75	76	77	78	79
60	61	62	63	64	65	66	67	68	69
50	51	52	53	54	55	56	57	58	59
40	41	42	43	44	45	46	47	48	49
30	31	32	33	34	35	36	37	38	39
20	21	22	23	24	25	26	27	28	29
10	11	12	13	14	15	16	17	18	19
0	1	2	3	4	5	6	7	8	9

Don't Buy a Hundred Chart

The best way to help your children master math is to get them involved in making their own learning tools. Work together to create a large hundred chart on construction paper or poster board. Make the squares big enough that you can mark them with pennies, blocks, Lego people, or small toy dinosaurs.

Or download Natural Math blogger Yelena McManaman's hundred chart poster, which shows the meaning of each number. Hang it on the wall, low enough that your preschool or early elementary student can see it easily. Talk about the patterns your child notices. If you print and cut out McManaman's individual cards, you can arrange them so the bigger numbers are higher up, as shown in the original blog post about her son's reaction to the poster.[†]

Many of the activities for older students use printable hundred charts as a game board or for coloring patterns. You can find a handy collection of printable charts in my free *Hundred Charts Galore!* printables file, which you can download from my publishing website Tabletop Academy Press.[‡]

If your child has trouble making the jump from one line to the next, elementary teacher Jessica Boschen suggests rolling a printed chart into a cylinder. Trim the margins off a 1–100 or 0–99 chart. Wrap the paper around so the end of each line meets the beginning of the next. Tape it together. Then roll another piece of paper and slip it inside the

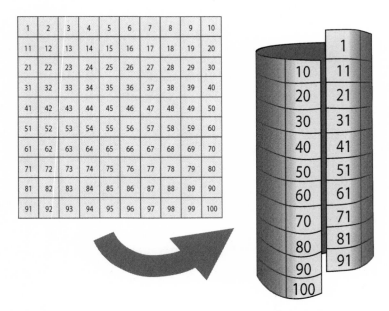

When you roll a hundred chart into a cylinder, children can easily follow the numbers from one row to the next.

† *MoebiusNoodles.com/2013/01/The-Hundred-Chart-And-Game-Cards*
naturalmath.com/2012/12/the-hundred-chart
‡ *tabletopacademy.net/free-printables*

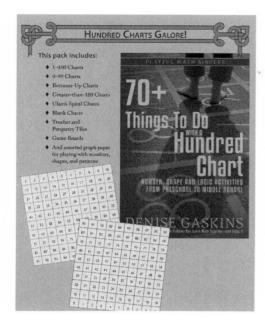

HUNDRED CHARTS GALORE!

This pack includes:

♦ 1–100 Charts
♦ 0–99 Charts
♦ Bottoms-Up Charts
♦ Greater-than-100 Charts
♦ Ulam's Spiral Charts
♦ Blank Charts
♦ Trischet and
  Parquetry Tiles
♦ Game Boards
♦ And assorted graph paper
  for playing with numbers,
  shapes, and patterns

Your children can play
with 1–100 charts,
0–99 charts, and
more with my free
printables file.

hundred chart for support. Center the chart on the paper and tape it in place.

Don't Stop at One Hundred

As your children grow, try a few of the activities in this book with charts that start and end at other numbers.

Malia Hollowell, founder of The STEM Laboratory website, explains the importance of using beyond-one-hundred charts: "Ask a first grader what number comes after 100 and you'll likely hear something like '110' or '200.' It can be confusing for new mathematicians to understand the patterns that happen after the number 100 if they don't see them."

I've included a few large-numbered charts in my printables pack. There's even a "hundred hundreds" chart that starts with 100, 200, 300 ... and goes to 10,000.

And with a page of blank squares, you can make any chart you can imagine. Remember, a hundred chart doesn't have to start with a *friendly number* (a number that's easy to work with). What if you label the first square 437 — where would your chart end? Would it go all the way to 537? Try it and see.

What if you started with a big number and counted down for each square?

What if you write a zero somewhere near the middle of your hundred chart? Which numbers would belong in the other squares? Do you notice anything funny about the rows and columns in this chart?

David Burns's Helping with Math website lets you generate charts that start at whatever number you specify and count by whichever interval you choose. You could make an even numbers chart, or a multiples-of-three chart, and so on. The possibilities are endless.[†]

Body-Scale Hundred Charts

Sometimes it's fun to go big, to get your child's whole body involved in playing with math patterns. Children's bodies link with their minds to form a holistic learning machine that can master abstract concepts through action.

"Allowing students' bodies to interact with this tool in a new way can deepen their understanding of its structure and inspire new insights about the relationship between the numbers within," says Malke Rosenfeld, author of *Math on the Move: Engaging Students in Whole Body Learning.* "We want math to make sense to our students, and the moving body is a wonderful partner toward that goal."

There are a variety of ways to create full-body hundred charts. Former teacher Megan Sheakoski drew a chart on clear contact paper and taped it to a window, sticky side out, so her kids could attach number cards and move them around. Reading specialist Lorie King Kaehler, author of *Chalk on the Wild Side,* wrote the numbers 1–100 on large Post-It sticky notes to create an interactive floor chart for her children. Elementary math coach Jenn Kranenburg made a giant chart on her classroom floor with masking tape. And mom blogger Terri

† *helpingwithmath.com/printables/tables_charts/1nbt1-numbers-chart01.htm*

Thompson surprised her kids with a sidewalk chalk hundred chart on the driveway.

How to Use This Book

In the following chapters, you'll find many ideas for playing with a hundred chart. Some activities will focus on the numbers of the chart. Others will explore different ways to manipulate the pattern of squares on a blank chart.

For several of the activities or games, you will need a printed chart, either numbered or blank. Be sure to download the free *Hundred Charts Galore!* file.

You may also need pencils or colored felt-tip markers, dice or playing cards, and game tokens for each player. If you make a hundred chart on poster board, small toys make fun tokens for young players. On printed charts, you can use colored glass gems from a craft store, bits of colored paper crumpled into balls, or small-diameter coins. In the U.S., pennies and nickels work well for two-player games because they're cheap and the coins are different colors.

I've organized the chapters by topic: counting, patterns, addition and subtraction, multiplication, and advanced concepts. Within each section, I've placed the activities that seemed easiest to me at the beginning, with the challenge level increasing as the chapter progresses.

But don't confuse this organization with a grade-level progression. Even in the "Basic Counting" section, you'll find a couple of activities to challenge middle school students. And young students may enjoy some of the logic games or math debates in Chapter Six.

And Most Important

Keep in mind the value of playing with math.

Never let an activity degenerate into performance assessment, a quiz or test of your child's abilities.

Play can be scary to those of us who grew up in an authoritarian school system where the student's job was to listen to the teacher and follow instructions. Being in control gives us adults security, and we fear letting it go.

What if an activity totally flops? What if we make a mistake?

What if our child finds out we don't know all the answers?

What if we ruin our children's education?

Perhaps it's melodramatic, but I've had all those fears many times in the course of homeschooling my kids and teaching my classes. Sometimes they aren't conscious thoughts, just a nervous feeling in my gut that says, "Don't take the risk!"

Activities do fail. We choose something that's too advanced for our students, or so easy it's boring. But that's okay. We can try something else tomorrow.

We do make mistakes, and that's a good thing. We can model for our kids how to respond to a mistake, how to recognize it as an opportunity to learn. If we never made mistakes, we would never grow.

And playing will never hurt our children's education. Play releases stress and gives children a positive attitude toward learning. It helps them build intuitive connections between topics. And it lays a solid groundwork on which later formal lessons can build.

While you play, carry on a conversation with your kids. Ask what they think, and then really listen. You'll be amazed at how often a child's fresh perspective can help you yourself understand math more deeply.

In several activities, I've included a few suggested discussion questions. These are only a sample of the ideas you and your child might explore. Some questions may seem to have a specific right or wrong answer, but the answer is never as important as the process of sharing ideas together. Thinking about the numbers or shapes. Noticing connections and wondering about relationships.

As retired math professor Herb Gross says, "What's really neat about mathematics is that even when there's only one right answer, there's never only one right way to do the problem."

Several places through the book, I suggest that your children experiment with their own modifications of the rules for a math game. But even where I don't mention it, feel free to tweak any activity. To make a small change and see how that affects other things is a playful, mathematical way of thinking.

Whenever possible, take turns with your child. Children love the chance to "boss" an adult—and this makes even a straight-forward activity feel like a game, not an educational chore.

Talk with your children. Listen to their thoughts.

And most of all, enjoy yourselves.

Author's Note: All the website links in this book were checked before publication, but the Internet is volatile. If a website disappears, you can run a browser search for the author's name or article title. Or enter the web address at the Internet Archive Wayback Machine.[†]

---

† *archive.org/web/web.php*

1	2	3	4	5	6	7	8	9	10
11	12	13	14	15	16	17	18	19	20
21	22	23	24	25	26	27	28	29	30
31	32	33	34	35	36	37	38	39	40
41	42	43	44	45	46	47	48	49	50
51	52	53	54	55	56	57	58	59	60
61	62	63	64	65	66	67	68	69	70
71	72	73	74	75	76	77	78	79	80
81	82	83	84	85	86	87	88	89	90
91	92	93	94	95	96	97	98	99	100

A hundred chart heart, from Activity #10 Picture Puzzles.
Give a clue for each number: "Color ten more than sixty-three.
The double of thirty. The number that's half of seventy …"

CHAPTER 2

Counting

You know what?
        Children like mathematics.
Children see the world mathematically.

When we do a puzzle,
        when we count things,
                when we see who's got more,
                        or who's taller.
Play and mathematics are not on opposite sides of the stage.

—DOUG CLEMENTS

Basic Counting

COUNTING BUILDS NUMBER SENSE AND prepares children for later math topics. Talk together as you count and play with numbers.

Introduce your child to vocabulary that describes the number positions and relationships. Use math words like above, below, right, left, up, down, next to, before, after, between, begins with, less than, greater than, least, greatest, row, and column.

— 1 —

Count Up

Use a handmade or printed number chart to practice counting.

With young children who have trouble moving from one line to the next, you may want to use the 1–50 Counting Chart from my *Hundred Charts Galore!* file.[†]

Adults tire of repetition, but children enjoy the rhythm of counting. Without realizing it, your kids will absorb the patterns that strengthen their intuition for how numbers work.

Count on the chart to a favorite number. Or count all the way to one hundred (or the greatest number on your chart).

Try choral counting, saying the numbers together.

Or alternate with your child, taking turns saying the numbers.

MATH TIDBIT: Did you know that the number you say when you point to each square has two meanings? It tells the order of that particular square in the counting sequence (*ordinal* number). And it also tells how many squares you have touched up to that point (*cardinal* number), if you started counting at one.

---

† *tabletopacademy.net/free-printables*

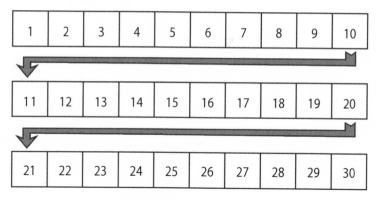

| 1 | 2 | 3 | 4 | 5 | 6 | 7 | 8 | 9 | 10 |

| 11 | 12 | 13 | 14 | 15 | 16 | 17 | 18 | 19 | 20 |

| 21 | 22 | 23 | 24 | 25 | 26 | 27 | 28 | 29 | 30 |

The 1–50 Counting Chart has paths to guide
children from one row to the next.

— 1.5 —

Count with Action Cards

You will need a hundred chart, a stack of blank index cards, one or two six-sided dice, and a Lego person or other small toy for each player.

Write simple actions like "Hop on one foot" and "Spin around" on the index cards, one action per card. Or download the printable action cards from Amy Mascott's Teach Mama website, or the cards from Rachel Capes's Wiggle to 100 game.[†]

Shuffle and stack your cards face down, or spread them into a "Go Fish" pond.

On your turn, roll the dice. Pick up a card and repeat the action as many times as the number you rolled. Then move your character that many spaces on the chart, saying aloud the number in each square you touch.

The first player to reach or pass one hundred wins. For a shorter game, choose a different target number.

---

† *teachmama.com/action-action-1-2-3*
youvegotthismath.com/2016/01/19/wiggle-to-100

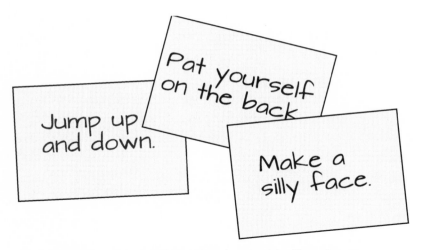

Children love having adults play along in this silly action game.

—2—

Count Down

Follow your chart backward to count down from the highest number.

Or count down starting from any number. Let your child pick the number you start at.

Most people find counting down harder than counting up. Are some numbers more confusing for your child than others?

—3—

Notice and Wonder

When you are counting with your child, ask: "What do you notice?"

Take turns mentioning simple things about the numbers in your chart.

"I notice seven."

"I see another seven here in twenty-seven."

"I see a number with two sevens."

"I notice ten."

"I notice that ten has a one and a zero."

"I see eight looks the same upside down."

And so on.

Learning to pay attention to what we see is a valuable skill. Too often, we skim through life without observing what is around us. But in math, taking the time to notice things can become a problem-solving tool.

Don't tell your children what you want them to see. Let them engage with the numbers directly. My kids almost never think about things the same way I would, and their comments often surprise and delight me.

Then ask your child, "What do you wonder?"

Take turns mentioning things that you wonder about numbers.

"I wonder how many sevens are in the whole chart."

"I wonder if there are numbers that aren't on our chart."

"I wonder what comes after one hundred."

"I wonder what's the biggest number?"

TEACHER's TIP: Don't feel like you have to explain the things your children notice or to answer their wonderings. The point of this activity is to begin building awareness of numbers and their patterns. You have many years of exploration ahead to learn about the logic behind those patterns.

— 4 —

Find the Number

This game gives your children a chance to show off how well they recognize numbers.

Call out a number and have your child cover it with a counter or tile. Plastic Bingo counters are great because they're colorful, but you can still see the number through them.

Take turns. Now your child gets to call a number for you to mark.

Rounding Up or Down

Use a 0–99 chart. Say a number. Your child puts a small toy, crumpled ball of colored paper, or other token on that number.

Then the child decides which multiple of ten is closest and slides the toy to that square. Is the number closer to the beginning of its own row? Or is it almost ready to jump to the next row?

For example, thirty-seven is between the squares for thirty and forty. But it's closer to forty. So we say, "Thirty-seven rounds up to forty."

Take turns. Now your child gets to say a number for you to round up or down.

You must make a decision when you get a number that ends in five. The somethingty-five numbers are exactly midway between their nearest multiples of ten.

Should we round them up or down?

Ask your children what they think.

20	21	22	23	24	25	26	27	28	29
30	31	32	33	34	35	36	37	38	39
40	41	42	43	44	45	46	47	48	49

Rounding is easy for children to see on a 0–99 chart. Is 37 close
friends with 30, or does it want to jump to the next row?

TEACHER'S TIP: The standard elementary school rule is to round somethingty-five numbers up to the next multiple of ten. But in real-world problems, that rule may not always apply. Let your kids decide what makes sense to them.

Rounding Bigger Numbers

You can find plenty of cute mnemonic class posters on the internet for almost any math topic, including how to round big numbers. These may look nice on a classroom wall, but most of them rely more on wordplay than on making sense of math. Avoid them.

Instead, teach your children to think about *what the numbers mean.*

Rounding is closely related to estimation. It's a way to simplify a number by thinking of a friendlier, easier-to-imagine number that names approximately the same amount of stuff. If you wanted to find out how rich Jeff Bezos is, you wouldn't really care about his pocket change — only the bigger place values would matter.

To figure out how to round large numbers, students can draw an open number line — that is, a line with no beginning or end — and put their number on it.

For instance, to round 1,237 to the nearest hundred, you would draw a horizontal line on a whiteboard or scratch paper.

Now you need to decide which hundred-numbers sit on either side of 1,237. If you ignore the "pocket change," which values are nearest your number? Make two marks near the ends of the open line and label them 1,200 and 1,300.

What number is exactly midway between these two? Mark the midpoint and label it 1,250.

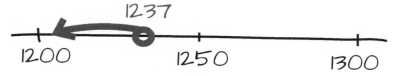

An open number line is any small chunk of the whole, infinite number line. You mark only the numbers you need to solve your problem.

Then think about the number you are trying to round. Is it more or less than 1,250? Mark it on the number line.

Finally, you are ready to answer the question: Which hundred number is closest?

— 6 —

Count Time

Mark one square per day to count how long you've been doing school or to keep track of summer vacation days.

Or count down to your child's birthday or another special occasion. How many days are left until the big day?

— 7 —

Count Money

Help your child learn the value of coins by counting with pocket change on the hundred chart. I use U.S. money in the examples below. Your coins may have different values, so adapt the investigation to fit your own currency.

Use a 1–100 chart, which represents one dollar's worth of value. One dollar is worth one hundred cents. Each time you fill the chart with any combination of coins that amount is worth one dollar.

It takes one hundred pennies (one-cent coins) to make one dollar. Each penny will cover one square.

A nickel is a five-cent coin. You can trade five squares' worth of pennies for a nickel.

Nickels count by fives. If you count nickels on the hundred chart, put them on the squares for five, ten, fifteen, and so on. How many nickels does it take to fill the chart? How many nickels make one dollar?

A dime is a ten-cent coin. You can trade ten squares' worth of coins (pennies or nickels) for a dime. Even though the U.S. dime is smaller than a penny or nickel, it's worth more.

Dimes count by tens. On the hundred chart, dimes go on the squares for ten, twenty, and so on. How many dimes make one dollar?

A quarter is a twenty-five-cent coin. Each quarter is one-fourth of a dollar.

What coins can you trade for a quarter? How many different ways can you make the value of a quarter with smaller coins?

How many quarters does it take to fill the chart? What number squares should you put them on?

Set a pile of coins on the table. Take turns picking up a handful of coins to count on the hundred chart.

Teacher's Tip: When counting coins, it's usually easiest to start with the larger denominations and work down to the pennies.

— 7.5 —

Make Change for a Dollar

The ability to count change has become a lost art. But it's still a good way to help children understand both math and money.

When you count change, you begin at the amount spent and count up to one hundred.

For example, imagine you are running a garage sale. Somebody buys a toy for thirty-two cents, but they give you a dollar. How much change should they get?

You could do a subtraction calculation on paper or with a calculator: one hundred minus thirty-two.

Or you could take advantage of two important mathematical facts:

(1) Subtraction and addition are closely related. Mathematicians call them *inverse operations*. That means you can use addition to solve a subtraction problem.

(2) Addition is closely related to counting. You can use counting to solve an addition problem.

To count change, we rely on these two principles. Here's how it works:

The buyer holds out a hand for their change. You count the coins as you place them into their palm.

First, you say the price of the toy: "Thirty-two."

Then you give enough pennies, one at a time, to get up to a multiple of five. Count aloud each penny as you set it down: "Thirty-three. Thirty-four. Thirty-five."

Next you give them a nickel, which brings the total up to a multiple of ten. You say, "Forty."

Set down a dime to bring the total up to "Fifty."

Now count by quarters the rest of the way. As you set down each quarter, count aloud the running total: "Seventy-five. One dollar."

Notice that when you count change, you don't have to do any subtraction. You never actually calculate the amount of change. You just count up to one hundred by the coin values.

Keep in mind that the counting rules are flexible. You do need at least a few pennies. But once you get up to a multiple of five, you can use the larger coins in whatever order makes sense to you.

For example, consider your garage sale possibilities. What if you looked in the coin box and discovered you're out of nickels? You could keep going with pennies all the way to forty, then continue with dimes as above. Or you could count by dimes after thirty-five: "Forty-five. Fifty-five. Sixty-five. Seventy-five." And then finish with a quarter.

Can you show what counting change looks like on the hundred chart?

Take turns naming a price for the other person to make change.

ADVANCED PUZZLE: What is the fewest number of coins you need to make change for any price up to a dollar? (For higher prices, you would need paper bills, too.) Dig into your pile of coins and play around a bit, trying different arrangements.

TEACHER'S TIP: See the Answers to Selected Problems at the end of the book—but only to check after you've decided on your own solution. A puzzle is no fun when someone just gives you the answer.

— 8 —

Count Data

Your child can use a blank hundred or 120 chart to make a simple bar or line graph to record data.

Make a *bar graph* when you are counting different categories or groups of items. Label each column (for vertical bars) or row (for horizontal bars) with the type of thing being counted. Then color or mark one square for each item.

If you are counting large collections, you may need to let each square represent two or more of the items. Discuss the appropriate *scale* (items per square) for your graph. What might happen if you didn't use a consistent scale?

Here are several ideas for bar graphs:

♦ Colors in a candy bag

♦ Birthday months of your family and friends

♦ How many pets your friends own

♦ Favorite foods or snacks

♦ Sizes of the other planets compared to Earth

♦ Probability: coin tosses or dice rolls

Make a *line graph* to show how something changes over time. Label the bottom of the chart with time (days of the week, perhaps) and the side of the chart with number values of the thing you are measuring. Again, you need to decide on the most useful scale for the graph, so the reader can see the variation and understand your data.

Here are some ideas for line graphs:

- Daily temperature or rainfall

- Minutes spent viewing TV or reading

- Money earned on chores or at a job

- Sport or hobby statistics

- Plant growth, or other science experiment

- Stock fluctuations (choose a pretend stock portfolio and follow your imaginary gains or losses online)

Talk about the importance of using a title and labels on your graph. Can a stranger look at your chart and tell exactly what it means, without you having to explain anything?

You can make a bar graph out of anything you can count.

Use physical objects or pictures to mark the squares, or just color them in.

My Bag of Candy

green · blue · red · yellow · orange · brown

High and Low Temperatures

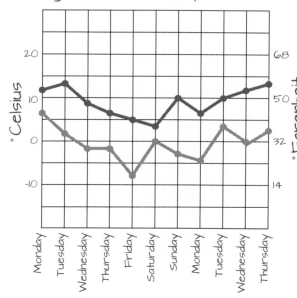

Line graphs show changes over time.

If you want people to understand your graph, be sure to label everything and use a consistent scale.

Population Balance in the Zombie Apocalypse

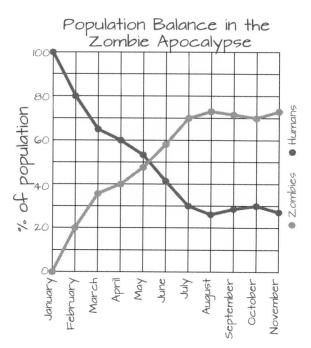

Counting Puzzles

— 9 —

Number Match

Use your favorite homemade hundred chart as a game board, or print a chart from my free printables file.

Print another hundred chart on card stock, and cut the number squares apart to make number tiles. It's fine if the tiles are smaller than the squares on your game board, as long as they have the same numbers.

If you want larger game tiles for young fingers, you can write numbers by hand on squares that fit your homemade hundred chart. Or make plastic game pieces by writing the numbers with a permanent marker on milk jug lids.

Mix all the tiles face down in a fishing pond. Take turns choosing a tile. Place it on the matching number square of your game board chart.

Or play free-for-all. Everyone picks and places numbers at the same time as fast as you can go.

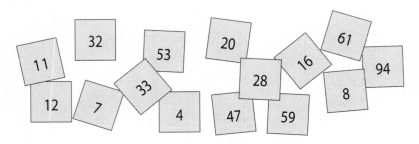

Number tiles are easy to make, and you can
use them in a variety of playful ways.

Cover your eyes while your child switches two or three of the number tiles. Can you find the "mistakes" and put them right? Now it's your turn to make some "mistakes" for your child to fix.

— 9.5 —

Scavenger Hunt

Use the chart and number tiles from Number Match.

Hide the number tiles around the house. Since there are so many tiles, you may want to put more than one in each hiding place.

Let your children search for the tiles and match them to your hundred chart.

— 10 —

Picture Puzzles

Give your child a printed number chart and colored felt-tip markers.

Then you give clues appropriate for your child's ability. Clues might be the number itself or a description of a number ("It's two less than twenty-six") or a math expression that equals the number.

Your child solves the clue and colors in the appropriate square.

Keep giving clues until the design is complete.

Now, let your child make up a puzzle for you to color.

— 11 —

Jigsaw Puzzles

Cut your choice of printed number chart into six or more irregular pieces (cut along the lines that separate the squares) to make a puzzle.

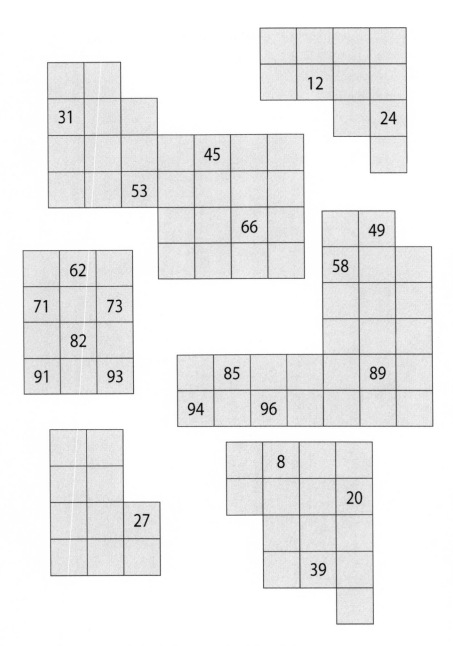

A hundred chart jigsaw puzzle. To make a tougher
challenge, include fewer number clues.

Can your child put the chart back together?

For younger children, offer a normal hundred chart as a base on which to arrange their pieces.

For a greater challenge, write a few numbers scattered around a blank chart. Cut it into puzzle pieces, making sure there's at least one number on each piece. Can your child fill in the rest of the numbers?

Elementary math coach Donna Boucher calls this type of puzzle a Humpty Dumpty hundred chart.

Counting Games

Your child may have already played the most famous hundred chart game, Snakes (or Chutes) and Ladders. Here are several new ways to play with numbers.

— 12 —

Speeding Car Game

two players, online download

Leah Hudson's "Stop the Speeding Car" is a two-player counting game for young children, racing on your favorite homemade hundred chart. You'll need a couple of small cars for the game pieces, and one or two dice.

Download the printable cards from her Simple Home Blessing blog.[†]

— 13 —

Push the Penny

two or more players, any chart

You will also need a deck of playing cards and one penny or other small token.

Remove the face cards and all the numbers greater than six from the deck. Or whatever number is very easy for your child to count, so the mechanics of the game go smoothly and your child can focus on

---

† *simplehomeblessing.com/preschool-math-game*

the hundred chart numbers.

Deal two cards to each player. Mix the remaining cards face down to make a fishing pond. Set the penny or other token on the first square of your chart.

Take turns moving the penny. On your turn, draw one card from the pond, so you have three numbers to choose from. Lay down one of your cards face up and push the penny that number of spaces up the chart.

But if your move would take the penny past the last square of the hundred chart, you have to count down instead. For example, imagine the penny is sitting on square ninety-eight. If you play a three, you can't push the penny forward because it would go off the chart. So you must count down to ninety-five.

Say the name of the number where you stopped. And then tell something you notice about that number.

Suppose you landed on ninety-five. You might say that it has a nine and a five in it. Or that it comes after ninety-four and before ninety-six. That it's in the same column as eighty-five, but one row farther on the chart. That it's bigger than seven. Or ... what would *you* see in ninety-five?

Turn the card you played face down and mix it back into the fishing pond. Then it's the next player's turn.

The player who lands the penny on the last square (ninety-nine or one hundred, depending on your chart) by exact count wins the game.

— 14 —

Dollar Derby

two or more players, printed charts

Players each need their own printed chart. You will also need one six-sided die (or two dice for a shorter game) and a large pile of assorted coins.

Set the coins in the middle of the table where everyone can reach.

Take turns rolling the die and collecting that many pennies. Place the pennies on your chart, one coin per square, counting up from the lowest number.

When you run out of pennies, use the money on your chart to make change for higher-value coins. For example, if you roll a three, you may take a nickel from the pile, as long as you give back two cents from your chart. Or you might take a quarter if you can make twenty-two cents in change.

The first player to collect a dollar's worth of coins (or more) wins the game.

— 15 —

The Nickel Game

two players or two teams, chart optional

Print your choice of number chart, or players may work mentally, agreeing on the range of numbers before play begins.

Give each player (or team) twenty nickels. Small tokens like dried beans or colored glass gems would also work, and you can even use crumpled bits of paper.

One player chooses a secret number on the chart, or within the agreed-upon range.

The second player makes a guess by placing a nickel on any square. Or if playing mentally, the player sets down a nickel and says the number aloud. The first player signals thumb-up if the secret number is greater than the guess or thumb-down if it is less.

Or you can practice math vocabulary. The first player can say, "My number is greater (or less) than [name the number guessed]."

The second player continues to guess with nickels until the secret number is revealed. The first player collects all the nickels on the board.

Then the second player chooses a number for the first one to guess, paying one nickel per guess as before.

Play an even number of games, so each player has the same number of chances to gather nickels. Whoever collects the most money is the champion.

— 16 —

The Number Puzzle Game

two to four players, online download

This game is a fun cross between the hundred chart jigsaw puzzle (#11 above) and the strategy game Gomoku (#66).

Each player needs his or her own printed hundred chart and a pencil, colored marker, or small tokens for marking squares.

The players each draw one card from a deck of cards marked with jigsaw puzzle pieces. Every card shows one number, and the rest of the squares are blank.

Players find the squares on their own hundred chart that match the card they drew. They choose just one of those squares and mark it by coloring or placing a token.

When all players have finished marking their square, discard those cards and draw new ones for the next turn.

The first player to mark five squares in a row wins the game.

VARIATION: For a more competitive game, all players share one chart and take turns marking their squares.

You can download a basic version of the card deck at Rachel Capes's You've Got This blog (free registration required). Or buy the complete set at Teachers Pay Teachers.[†]

[†] *youvegotthismath.com/2016/07/27/numberpuzzlegame*
teacherspayteachers.com/Product/Number-Puzzle-Games-with-Boards-from-100-to-900-2692535

Activity #22: Truchet Tile Patterns. These are from Sebastien
Truchet's original paper "Mémoire sur les combinaisons" (1704).

CHAPTER 3

Patterns

What humans do
> *with the language of mathematics*
>> *is to describe patterns.*

To grow mathematically
> *children must be exposed*
>> *to a rich variety of patterns*
>>> *appropriate to their own lives*
>> *through which they can see variety,*
> *regularity,*
>> *and interconnections.*

—LYNN ARTHUR STEEN

Number Patterns

COUNTING IS NOT THE ONLY way to build number sense. Patterns are interesting, and they prepare children for multiplication and for algebra. Encourage your students to think often and deeply about patterns.

If you're like me, the word "pattern" makes you think of shapes and designs. But interesting patterns appear in numbers as well. Noticing these number patterns and thinking about why they happen will strengthen your child's understanding of math.

— 17 —

Travel Patterns

We'll look at several math-fact patterns later, as we explore addition and multiplication. But for now, let's focus on patterns created by the numbers themselves.

Walk your finger straight across the chart and pay attention to the numbers you pass. What pattern do you see when you travel along a row? Up a column?

How do the numbers change when your finger walks down a diagonal? Up a diagonal?

What if you take a zigzag path?

How will you travel through the numbers?

— 18 —

Digit Patterns

Use colored paper squares, translucent plastic Bingo chips, or other small tokens to mark patterns in the numbers on your favorite homemade hundred chart. Or print several paper charts and use colored pencils or felt-tip markers to shade in the squares.

If you have my free *Hundred Charts Galore!* printables file, you can use the multi-chart pages to see more patterns at a glance.[†]

Mark all the numbers with a seven in them. Why do they make that shape?

Mark the numbers whose digits add up to ten. What shape do they make?

Mark the numbers with double digits, like twenty-two and thirty-three.

On a single chart, mark all the numbers with a four in them *and* all the numbers whose digits add up to four. Isn't that a cool trick?

What other number patterns can you find?

0	1	2	3	4	5	6	7	8	9
10	11	12	13	14	15	16	17	18	19
20	21	22	23	24	25	26	27	28	29
30	31	32	33	34	35	36	37	38	39
40	41	42	43	44	45	46	47	48	49
50	51	52	53	54	55	56	57	58	59
60	61	62	63	64	65	66	67	68	69
70	71	72	73	74	75	76	77	78	79
80	81	82	83	84	85	86	87	88	89
90	91	92	93	94	95	96	97	98	99

0	1	2	3	4	5	6	7	8	9
10	11	12	13	14	15	16	17	18	19
20	21	22	23	24	25	26	27	28	29
30	31	32	33	34	35	36	37	38	39
40	41	42	43	44	45	46	47	48	49
50	51	52	53	54	55	56	57	58	59
60	61	62	63	64	65	66	67	68	69
70	71	72	73	74	75	76	77	78	79
80	81	82	83	84	85	86	87	88	89
90	91	92	93	94	95	96	97	98	99

0	1	2	3	4	5	6	7	8	9
10	11	12	13	14	15	16	17	18	19
20	21	22	23	24	25	26	27	28	29
30	31	32	33	34	35	36	37	38	39
40	41	42	43	44	45	46	47	48	49
50	51	52	53	54	55	56	57	58	59
60	61	62	63	64	65	66	67	68	69
70	71	72	73	74	75	76	77	78	79
80	81	82	83	84	85	86	87	88	89
90	91	92	93	94	95	96	97	98	99

0	1	2	3	4	5	6	7	8	9
10	11	12	13	14	15	16	17	18	19
20	21	22	23	24	25	26	27	28	29
30	31	32	33	34	35	36	37	38	39
40	41	42	43	44	45	46	47	48	49
50	51	52	53	54	55	56	57	58	59
60	61	62	63	64	65	66	67	68	69
70	71	72	73	74	75	76	77	78	79
80	81	82	83	84	85	86	87	88	89
90	91	92	93	94	95	96	97	98	99

0	1	2	3	4	5	6	7	8	9
10	11	12	13	14	15	16	17	18	19
20	21	22	23	24	25	26	27	28	29
30	31	32	33	34	35	36	37	38	39
40	41	42	43	44	45	46	47	48	49
50	51	52	53	54	55	56	57	58	59
60	61	62	63	64	65	66	67	68	69
70	71	72	73	74	75	76	77	78	79
80	81	82	83	84	85	86	87	88	89
90	91	92	93	94	95	96	97	98	99

0	1	2	3	4	5	6	7	8	9
10	11	12	13	14	15	16	17	18	19
20	21	22	23	24	25	26	27	28	29
30	31	32	33	34	35	36	37	38	39
40	41	42	43	44	45	46	47	48	49
50	51	52	53	54	55	56	57	58	59
60	61	62	63	64	65	66	67	68	69
70	71	72	73	74	75	76	77	78	79
80	81	82	83	84	85	86	87	88	89
90	91	92	93	94	95	96	97	98	99

Print a page with several small hundred charts so
you can mark and compare different patterns.

---

† *tabletopacademy.net/free-printables*

No Sharing

Use colored paper squares, translucent plastic Bingo chips, or other small tokens to mark squares on your favorite hundred chart.

Can you mark ten squares with tokens so that no two of them share the same row or column?

If you play chess, think of this as a ten-rooks puzzle. How could you place ten rook pieces on a 10 × 10 "chessboard" so that all of them are safe?

Add up the numbers under your tokens to find your score for that pattern.

Can you find a different set of ten No-Sharing squares? What is the score for your new pattern?

What do you notice?

Does it make you wonder?

After you mark one square, no other token can share that row or column.

Following this rule, how many tokens can you fit onto your hundred chart?

1	2	3	4	5	6	7	8	9	10
11	12	13	14	15	16	17	18	19	20
21	22	23	24	25	26	27	⬤	29	30
31	32	33	34	35	36	37	38	39	40
41	42	43	44	45	46	47	48	49	50
51	52	53	54	55	56	57	58	59	60
61	62	63	64	65	66	67	68	69	70
71	72	73	74	75	76	77	78	79	80
81	82	83	84	85	86	87	88	89	90
91	92	93	94	95	96	97	98	99	100

Shape Patterns

— 20 —

Name Patterns

Print a blank hundred chart or draw a grid of squares on paper or a whiteboard.

Write your name in the squares. Start in the first square and write one letter per box. When you get to the last letter in your name, start over in the next square.

How many of you will fit in the hundred chart?

Color the first letter of your name each time it appears. What pattern does it make?

Try making patterns with other words.

What do you notice?

— 21 —

Pattern Machine

Print a blank hundred or 120 chart on card stock. Cut sheets of colored paper into square tiles that fit on the chart.

Arrange the tiles to make any design against the background chart. Then arrange them a different way. And then another.

Try symmetrical patterns. Try asymmetrical patterns. Which do you prefer?

What's the simplest pattern you can think of?

What's the most intricate pattern?

Can you make a pattern that no one would expect?

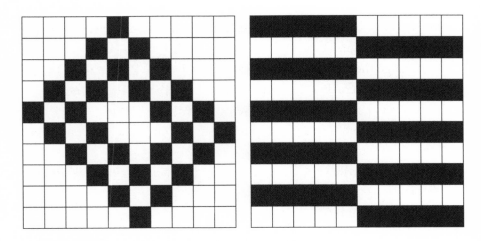

When children play with patterns, they think about symmetry, angles, and geometric transformations in a playful, creative way.

Would you like to make bigger designs? Print four blank charts and tape them together to create a large game board.

Leave the pattern machine (the blank hundred chart and colored square tiles) out on a convenient table for anyone to play with.

Teacher's Tip: You may be tempted to laminate the chart and tiles, but that will make your pattern slide out of place at the tiniest nudge. Friction is your friend.

Or get a plastic multiplication machine and cover the numbers with vinyl tape to make Christopher Danielson's original pattern machine.[†]

— 22 —

Truchet Tile Patterns

On card stock, print the Truchet tiles from my *Hundred Charts Galore!* printables file. Print a blank chart for a background, if desired.

Truchet tiles seem simple—a basic square cut in two parts along

---

† *christopherdanielson.wordpress.com/2016/03/11/the-sequence-machine*
linescurvesspirals.blogspot.co.uk/2018/02/diy-pattern-maker.html

the diagonal, half white and half black. Yet they can be arranged into amazingly complex designs.

Arrange the tiles to make any design against the background chart. Or spread the Truchet tiles out on a table to make larger patterns.

Rearrange the tiles into a different pattern.

Leave the tiles out for your family to play with. Take pictures of your favorite designs.

Search for Truchet tile images online and enjoy the patterns other people have created.

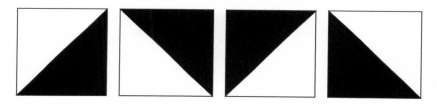

A single Truchet tile may be placed in one of four positions. With two tiles, there are sixteen permutations — or more, if you consider both vertical and horizontal positions. How many can you find?

— 22.5 —

Parquetry Patterns

In addition to the Truchet tiles above, print a sheet or two of black and white squares.

Parquetry (or *parquet*) is a geometric mosaic of light and dark wood pieces used for decorative effect, often as flooring or on a countertop or table.

Our parquetry patterns are less expensive than using real wood, yet full of possibilities for creative play. By adding square pieces to the basic set of Truchet tiles, we can make a nearly infinite variety of designs.

The thick lines act as mirrors.

Whatever you see on one side of the line, copy its reflection on the other side.

If you do it right, both of these puzzles will create the same design.

Symmetry Challenge

Each player will need a printed blank chart. Draw a line that divides the page in half. Your line may be vertical, horizontal, or diagonal.

Or draw two lines that split the chart into fourths. With two lines of symmetry, the pattern will match in both directions: top reflects bottom, and left reflects right.

With felt-tip markers or colored pencils, draw lines or fill in squares to make a pattern in one section (half or fourth) of your chart.

Trade papers with a friend. Can you complete each other's puzzle? Whatever shapes you see on one side of a mirror line, draw their reflections on the other side.

ADVANCED PUZZLE: Color shapes in different sections of the chart. Your shapes should not match each other symmetrically, but when all of them have been reflected across the line(s) of symmetry, they will create a finished design.

Curve Stitching

Mary Everest Boole invented curve stitching as a gentle introduction to geometric concepts in her 1904 book *The preparation of the child for science.*

On a printed blank chart, number the *intersections*—the places where lines meet—along the top from one (top left corner) to ten (next-to-last). Skip the top right corner, and then number the intersections down the right-hand side from one (just below the corner) to ten (bottom right corner).

With a ruler to draw straight lines, connect each pair of matching numbers.

What do you notice?

Create your own curves by numbering other lines on the chart and connecting points.

How can you change the curve?

What happens if the points are closer together? Or farther apart?

What happens if you use points on a diagonal line?

Or if the two lines cross each other?

When you find a design you like, turn it into string art. Transfer the numbered lines to card stock, and then stitch the curve with colored string.

MATH TIDBIT: Curve-stitching patterns are related to calculus. In differential calculus, we learn about curves by investigating the straight lines *tangent* to those curves—that is, the lines that skim along the edge of the curve, hitting just a single point.

Curves that we *create* using their tangent lines, as in curve stitching, are called *Bézier curves*. They serve as the basis for all sorts of computer graphics and animation.

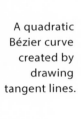

A quadratic Bézier curve created by drawing tangent lines.

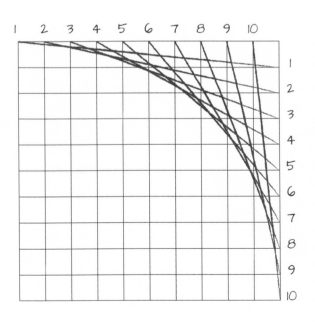

Pattern Games

— 25 —

Square Nim

two players or two teams, printed chart

You will need a blank hundred chart and a pencil, pen, or marker. Draw lines to divide the chart into five sets of twenty squares each, to make five games.

Each game is played in one set of twenty squares.

Take turns going first. On your turn, you must mark one square, and you may take up to four squares. The player who marks the last square of the set wins that game.

Nim is a simple game, so it's easy for children to think of new ways to play.

How will you modify the rules?

TEACHER'S TIP: Of all the games in the world, I think the math strategy game Nim has the most variations. For another example, look at #42 Hundred Chart Nim.

One theme ties together all Nim games: taking away pieces from a group. In this version, we start with a group of squares. In Hundred Chart Nim, a group of numbers.

Traditionally, it's a *misère* game, which means the player who takes the last item loses. My math club students call this the "poison" variation and enjoy acting dramatic death scenes when they lose the game.[†]

---

† *denisegaskins.com/2007/07/19/math-club-nim*

Connect Four

two players or two teams, printed chart

You will need a blank hundred or 120 chart and two different colored pencils — one for each player or team — plus a sturdy eraser for correcting mistakes. Define the number values of the chart by writing (in a non-player color) a number in one of the corner squares.

Play like Tic-Tac-Toe, with players (or teams) alternating to claim a square. But instead of using X and O to mark the squares, you mark the number value that belongs there.

For example, if you wrote the initial value 73 in the top left square, then a player might claim the square directly below that by adding ten and writing in "83."

Each time you get four squares in a row of your own color — horizontal, vertical, or diagonal — draw a line through them and add a point to your score tally.

Marked squares may not be counted again in another line going the same direction, but they can be part of a line that crosses the first.

When players discover mistakes, they may erase and correct the numbers without losing their squares.

Play until the board is filled with numbers or until no more new lines are possible.

Whoever draws the most four-in-a-row lines wins.

FOR BEGINNERS: Stick to the familiar hundred chart layout of numbers. You may want to fill in some "wild card" numbers scattered around the chart before starting the game. Wild squares may be used in a line by either player.

FOR A CHALLENGE: Try the game with three players using three different colors. Connect three squares in a row for each point.

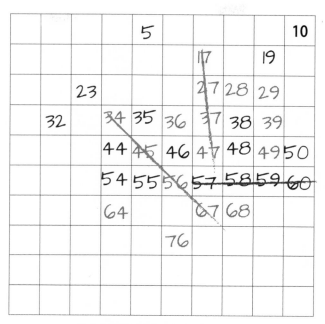

Connect Four game in progress.

TEACHER'S TIP: This game was invented by elementary school math specialist Joe Schwartz. Read his blog post to see the game variations his students suggested. How would your kids change the rules to make up their own related game?[†]

— 27 —

Battleship

two players or two teams, printed charts

Print two copies of the hundred chart for each player (or team). Or use the Battleship game board from my *Hundred Charts Galore!* printables file. You will also need pencils or felt-tip markers.[‡]

---

† *exit10a.blogspot.com/2016/01/i-like-this-game-because-you-have-to.html*
‡ *tabletopacademy.net/free-printables*

You may want to laminate the game boards and play with dry-erase markers.

Players must sit back-to-back or use something tall (like a science fair display board) to block their view of each other's boards.

One of your hundred charts is for your own ships. On the printable game board, this chart is labeled "My Fleet." Color squares to represent your ships floating in the sea. Each ship is a certain number of squares in a horizontal row or vertical column — no diagonals.

- ◆ Aircraft Carrier: five squares

- ◆ Battleship: four squares

- ◆ Cruiser: three squares

- ◆ Submarine: three squares

- ◆ Destroyer: two squares

The other hundred chart is your radar screen, on which you will search for the enemy fleet. Don't mark anything on it yet.

When both players have positioned their ships, you're ready to play. Take turns "firing shots" by saying a number on the hundred chart.

If the other player says a number where you have a ship, reply with "Hit" and mark an X over your ship on that square. If the player's shot doesn't hit one of your ships, that's a "Miss."

After a ship gets hit, it can still fight on. But if all the squares of that ship are hit, it sinks. Tell your opponent, "You've sunk my Cruiser." (Or whichever ship it was.)

On your turn to say a number, the other player will tell you whether it's a hit or a miss. Keep track of your shots by marking X's on your radar screen, and color in the squares where a shot hits something. You'll want to keep firing around that area until you sink the ship.

When all of one player's ships have been sunk, the game is over, and the other player wins.

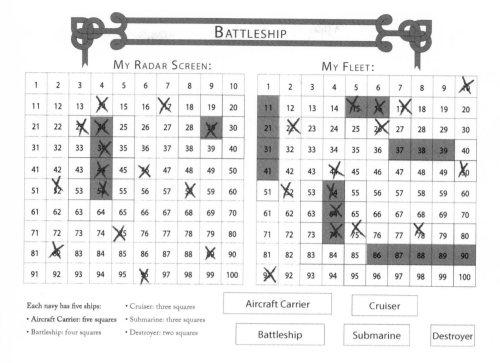

BATTLESHIP

MY RADAR SCREEN:

1	2	3	4	5	6	7	8	9	10
11	12	13	X	15	16	X	18	19	20
21	22	X	X	25	26	27	28	X	30
31	32	33	X	35	36	37	38	39	40
41	42	43	X	45	X	47	48	49	50
51	X	53	X	55	56	57	X	59	60
61	62	63	64	65	66	67	68	69	70
71	72	73	74	X	76	77	78	79	80
81	X	83	84	85	86	87	88	X	90
91	92	93	94	95	X	97	98	99	100

MY FLEET:

1	2	3	4	5	6	7	8	9	X
11	12	13	14	X	X	X	18	19	20
21	X	23	24	25	X	27	28	29	30
31	32	33	34	35	36	37	38	39	40
41	42	43	X	45	46	47	48	49	X
51	X	53	X	55	56	57	58	59	60
61	62	63	X	65	66	67	68	69	70
71	72	73	X	X	76	77	X	79	80
81	82	83	84	85	86	87	88	89	90
X	92	93	94	95	96	97	98	99	100

Each navy has five ships:
- Aircraft Carrier: five squares
- Battleship: four squares
- Cruiser: three squares
- Submarine: three squares
- Destroyer: two squares

Aircraft Carrier	Cruiser

Battleship	Submarine	Destroyer

You sank the battleship (four squares long), but the enemy
has sunk two of your ships. You just hit a new target at
square twenty-nine. Where will you aim your next shot?

Alternative Version: Hide-and-Seek Zoo

If your family prefers nonviolent play, you can replace the traditional
Battleship scenario with a story about zoo animals playing a game of
hide and seek.

Each player will hide the following animals:

♦ Elephant: five squares

♦ Giraffe: four squares

♦ Lion: three squares

♦ Alligator: three squares

♦ Chimpanzee: two squares

Play as in traditional Battleship, but instead of taking shots players name a chart square to "peek" at that position.

If the other player says a number where you've hidden an animal, answer "You see something" and mark an X over your animal on that square. If you want, you may get more specific: "There's a tail," or "You see an ear," or "Watch out for those teeth!" But if there's no animal in that square, reply "Nothing there."

When the other player uncovers all the squares for one of your animals, say, "You found my [name the animal]."

— 27.5 —

Salvo

two players or two teams, printed charts

Salvo is a faster version of the Battleship game. Play as above, except that players each get as many shots per turn as they have ships afloat. Or in the zoo variation, as many peeks as they have animals still hiding.

You and your opponent take all your shots at once before hearing the result. So you will probably want scratch paper to write down the numbers.

After all the shots are fired, players tell the hits and misses to each other and report whether any ships have sunk.

Then the next *salvo* (round of firing artillery) begins.

CHAPTER 4

Addition and Subtraction

Games teach or reinforce many of the skills
that a formal curriculum teaches,
plus one skill that formal teaching
sometimes leaves out—
the skill of having fun with math,
of thinking hard and enjoying it.

—PEGGY KAYE

Advanced Counting

IN THE BEGINNING, CHILDREN DO addition by counting up and subtraction by counting down. As they gain more experience, children learn to recognize patterns that make calculations easier.

Help your child notice relationships between numbers using words like both, total, all together, part, whole, put together, take apart, take away, combine, compare, more, fewer, increase, and decrease.

Practice math words such as tens digit, ones digit, plus, minus, equal, and not equal. The *sum* is the answer when you add two or more numbers. The *difference* is the answer when you subtract one number from another because subtracting tells you how far apart the numbers are.

— 28 —

Count More and Less

Use the chart like a number line to find numbers that are one more or one less than a given number. Ten more or ten less. Twenty more or less, and so on.

Count other addition (more than) and subtraction (less than) puzzles on your hundred chart. Take turns making up more-than and less-than problems for each other to solve.

TEACHER'S TIP: Children often find math easier to understand when they work with numbers in the same order they say them: biggest part first. Build mental math skills by showing how to add or subtract the tens first (counting up or down) and then the ones (counting left or right).

Can you find other mental math shortcut patterns? For instance, when you want to add nine, you may count along nine squares. But you could also add ten and then count backward one square. Which is easier?

— 29 —

Estimation

Use round numbers to estimate quickly the answers to addition and subtraction puzzles. No "borrowing" or "carrying" allowed!

What is 29 + 53? That's tough, but it's close to 30 + 50.

What is 34 + 67? Round it off to 30 + 70.

Take turns making up problems for each other to estimate.

Try your hand at a few estimating challenges, like the puzzles on Andrew Stadel's Estimation 180 website.[†]

— 30 —

Arrow Codes

Create arrow code puzzles. On your paper or whiteboard, write the starting number and several arrows. Each arrow tells you to move one square in the direction indicated.

What number is:

$$\text{“45} \leftarrow \leftarrow \uparrow \rightarrow \uparrow \text{”?}$$

How would you use arrows to write, "Start at twenty-seven and move to fifty-nine"?

How would you write, "Start at ninety-eight and subtract thirty-four"?

Take turns. Now your child gets to make up an arrow code for you to follow.

---

† *estimation180.com*

Number Bonds

A *number bond* is a mental picture of the relationship between a number and the parts that combine to make it.

Imagine a pile of six blocks, pebbles, or buttons. Then imagine separating them into two smaller piles. You might make piles of four and two, for example. How many different ways can you split your pile?

Number bonds help children understand the inverse relationship between addition and subtraction. Subtraction is not a totally different thing from addition; they are mirror images of the same idea. Addition is when you know the two smaller piles and want to find the total number of items. Subtraction is when you know the total, and you know one of the smaller piles, so you are trying to figure out the other set.

Young children need to handle physical blocks or stones, but older children can use their imagination.

Choose a target number such as ten, fifty, or one hundred. That will be your total number of imaginary items.

Then take turns pointing on the hundred chart to any number less than or equal to that target. The other player has to say how many more it takes to make the target number.

You can even point to numbers larger than the target. In that case, the number bond partner will be a negative number.

You can pull the six blocks apart into smaller piles. Then you can push them back together and split a different way.

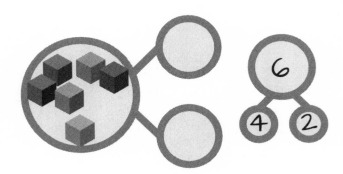

TEACHER'S TIP: With number bonds, our goal is not for children to memorize specific math facts. Rather, we want them to master the concept of taking a number apart and then putting it back together in different ways—an important foundation for understanding math.

Your children may enjoy playing a number bond game like Tens Concentration.[†]

—32—

Counting Revisited

How many numbers are there from 11 to 25? Are you sure?

What does it mean to count from one number to another? Does it include the first number, or the last one, or both, or neither?

Talk about *inclusive* and *exclusive* counting.

Then make up counting puzzles for each other.

MATH TIDBIT: When you are dealing with a real-life situation (or coding with arrays or loops) beware the *fencepost problem* (or *off-by-one error*). When people count how many days until an event, they usually skip today but include the final day in their count. But sometimes the things you want to count are like fence posts, and you need to include one at each end. And other times, what you care about are the spans in between the endpoints.

For example, if each span is eight feet, how many posts do you need to build a fence eighty feet long? Did you remember to count a post at each end?

Counting is harder than most people think!

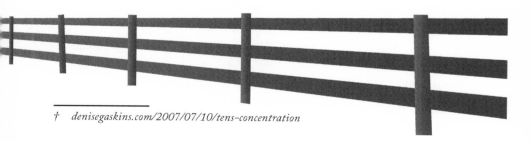

† *denisegaskins.com/2007/07/10/tens-concentration*

Sums and Differences

— 33 —

More Number Patterns

Use translucent plastic Bingo chips or other small tokens to mark addition and subtraction patterns on your favorite homemade hundred chart.

Or print several paper charts and use colored pencils to fill in the squares. Color lightly, so you can still read the numbers.

If you have my *Hundred Charts Galore!* printables file, you can use the multi-chart pages to see more patterns at a glance.

Mark the answer to 3 + 9=? Now go to 23 + 9, 33 + 9, 63 + 9.

What do you notice?

What's similar about 15 – 7, 25 – 7, 45 – 7, and so on?

What other addition and subtraction patterns can you find?

— 34 —

Next-Door Neighbors

Ask your child to choose any two next-door neighbor numbers—that is, two numbers in side-by-side squares—but not to tell you which ones. Then the child should add the numbers and tell you the sum.

Can you show off your magical skills by identifying the original numbers? Just subtract one from the sum, and then divide that new number in half to find the smaller of your child's two neighbor numbers.

It may take several tries for children to figure out this trick. After they get it, take turns adding neighbor numbers for the other person to guess.

Do you notice a pattern in the next-door neighbor sums? Will the total always be odd? Why, or why not?

What will happen if you add two apartment-house neighbors (one number above the other)—will the answer still be odd? Can you think of a "magic trick" pattern to identify the original numbers from their sum?

What about two numbers that sit diagonal to each other, touching at a corner?

TEACHER'S TIP: You can find answers in the back of the book. Don't peek. Nobody likes a spoiler.

— 35 —

Column Jumping

Choose any column of the hundred chart to study. For example, the threes column: 3, 13, 23, and so on.

Pick any two numbers in that column and add them together. In which column will you find the sum?

Try a different pair of numbers. Does their sum land in the same column?

What if the numbers are so big they go off your chart, like 73 + 93? Will the pattern still work? How can you tell?

What happens if you add four of the threes-column numbers together? Where do you find *that* sum?

How many threes-column numbers do you have to add for the sum to land in the eights column? Does it matter which numbers you pick?

Make a chart of the column jumping pattern for the threes. If you add enough threes-column numbers, can you get to each of the other columns?

Examine other column jumping patterns.

How many fours-column numbers do you have to add to land back

If I add this many numbers:	My sum will land in this column:
2	sixes
3	nines
4	twos
. . .	. . .

A chart of column jumps for numbers in the threes column.

in the fours column?

Can you add fours-column numbers and end up in the sevens? Why not?

What is the column jumping pattern for the tens?

Can you think of a way to predict the pattern for any numbers?

Do you think column jumping works for subtraction? It's easy to understand "add four of the numbers in the threes column." But what might it mean to "subtract four of the numbers"?

What happens when you subtract one threes-column number from another one? In which column will the difference land?

What if you subtract a big number from a smaller one — would the pattern extend into negative numbers?

— 36 —

Line Patterns

Find three numbers that touch each other to make a three-in-a-row line in any direction. Add them together. What is their sum?

Do you notice anything special about the sum? Try it with small numbers first because that makes it easier to see the pattern.

What happens when you add five numbers in a row?

What happens if you add four numbers in a row?

How is an even-length line different from an odd-length line?

Can you predict the line pattern sum for any line?

— 37 —

Cross and X Patterns

The cross pattern for any number is that square plus the four squares up, down, left, and right from it. The X pattern is that square plus the four touching it diagonally.

Pick any square that is not on the edge of your chart. Find its cross and X patterns.

Add up the sum of the numbers in the cross pattern.

Add up the sum of the numbers in the X pattern.

What do you notice?

Does it make you wonder?

Find the cross and X pattern sums for a different number.

Can you explain why the cross and X patterns for your square both add up to the same number? Will this always be true?

Find other patterns that work this way. Hint: Think about symmetry.

Can you predict the cross or X pattern sum for any number?

— 37.5 —

Calendar Patterns

Find the line, cross, or X patterns for a date on this month's calendar. Add up their sums.

How are these patterns the same as on a hundred chart?

How are they different?

Pentomino Sums

Pentominoes are five-square "dominoes." As with ordinary dominoes, we create pentominoes by joining squares by their sides.

[Did you think of the traditional domino tile game, with dots on the squares? For this activity, we only care about the shape of the tiles, not the number of dots.]

Unlike ordinary dominoes, which are all identical, pentominoes come in different shapes. There's only one way you can put two squares together to make a domino. But when there are five squares to play with, you have a lot more options.

Print a few blank charts on card stock. Ask your children to color the squares in groups of five, touching side-to-side (not just at a corner). How many arrangements can they make?

Cut out the designs and check for duplicates. If your children can rotate or flip one shape to match another, those two shapes are the same pentomino.

Did they find all twelve pentomino shapes?

Now print a regular hundred chart and try some puzzles. Can you fit all twelve pentominoes on a single hundred chart? Make sure each pentomino square fits exactly over a number square.

Can you arrange all twelve pentominoes into a tight rectangle, with no blank squares between them?

Pick one pentomino and set it anywhere on your hundred chart. What is the sum of the numbers covered by your pentomino?

Can you move your pentomino to another spot and cover the same total? Can you cover the same sum with a different pentomino?

Take turns making up puzzles for each other by naming a pentomino and a sum to cover. For example: "Use the Y to cover a total of 68."

Can you prove that the sum of numbers covered by the X pentomino will always equal five times the center square? Can you find similar rules for any of the other pentomino sums?

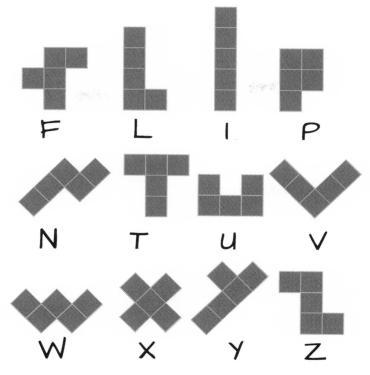

The twelve pentominoes, with their standard letter names.

Check My Math: I believe the "I" pentomino is the only other with a consistent sum — again, five times the central number — because all the others can be rotated in different directions. But I may be mistaken. If you find another pattern, I'd love to hear it.[†]

— 39 —

Palindrome Patterns

You will need a printed hundred or 120 chart, colored pencils or felt-tip markers, and scratch paper for written calculations.

In the margin of your hundred chart, make a color key. Write the numbers 0, 1, 2, 3, 4, and 5. Next to each number, scribble a swatch

---

† *LetsPlayMath@gmail.com*

of a different color. Add one more color swatch labeled "more than 5."

If you're using the higher-numbered chart, you may want to expand your key to include more color-numbers.

Use the zero color to shade in all the squares with single-digit numbers. Also shade the numbers where both digits are the same, like 33.

These numbers are *palindromes*—that is, they are the same forward and backward.

Now you are going to turn the remaining numbers into palindromes by the following rule:

- ◆ Write the number on scratch paper.

- ◆ Below it, write the number with the digits in reverse order.

- ◆ Add these two numbers together.

- ◆ If the sum is a palindrome, stop. If not, reverse the new number's digits and add again.

For example, seventy-eight takes four steps to make a palindrome:

$$78 + 87 = 165$$
$$165 + 561 = 726$$
$$726 + 627 = 1353$$
$$1353 + 3531 = 4884$$
Palindrome!

Color each number's square based on how many times you had to reverse-and-add to reach a palindrome.

Beware the tricky numbers 89 and 98. They will keep you busy for a long time.

What patterns do you notice?

Will every number transform itself into a palindrome if you keep going long enough?

MATH TIDBIT: That last question is one of the many unsolved problems in mathematics. Mathematicians don't know the answer. Some *conjecture* that all numbers will eventually reach a palindrome, others that they won't. Nobody has been able to prove it either way.

But for some numbers — like 196 — they haven't yet found a palindrome. Not even the guy who used a computer to do more than two million reverse-and-add calculations.

Does that make you wonder?

— 40 —

Sequences

Make up a secret rule for a pattern *sequence* — that is, a pattern where the numbers come in a particular order.

For example, you might start at fifty-five and add three at a time: 55, 58, 61, 64, and so on.

Mark the first three or four numbers of your sequence. Can your child name the next few numbers in the pattern?

Take turns. Now your child gets to mark a sequence for you to follow.

TEACHER'S TIP: Sometimes, the person guessing may think of a different rule than you had in mind for your sequence. That's fine, as long as their pattern makes sense. In math, there are often many right answers to a problem.[†]

---

† *denisegaskins.com/2015/08/03/math-with-many-right-answers*

Addition and Subtraction Games

— 41 —

Race to 100

two or more players, any chart

You will also need a deck of playing cards and a small toy or token for each player. Place tokens on the first square of the chart.

Take turns drawing a card from the deck. Number cards represent their face value, aces are worth one, and the face cards count as J = 11, Q = 12, K = 13.

Add the value of your card to the number of the square your token is sitting on. Say the answer out loud. If all players agree your sum is correct, move your token ahead to that new position.

The first person to reach or pass one hundred (or the greatest number on your chart) wins the game.

OPTIONAL RULE 1: You have to land on the final number by exact count. If your move would put you off the chart, you have to move backward (subtract) instead of forward.

OPTIONAL RULE 2: Before play, choose a category of squares—for example, numbers that end in seven or numbers with repeated digits (like forty-four)—that are "poison." If you land on a poison square, you have to go back to the beginning.

— 41.5 —

Race to Zero

two or more players, any chart

Same rules as Race to 100, except you start at the largest number on the chart. On each turn, subtract the number on your card from your current position, and move down toward zero.

— 42 —

Hundred Chart Nim

two players or two teams, chart optional

The first few times you play, use a number chart and small tokens, like dried beans or crumpled balls of paper. Both players use the same set of tokens.

The first player chooses any number from one to fifteen and places a token on that square of the number chart.

On your turn, you add five, ten, or fifteen to the most recently marked number. Place a new token on your sum.

Play alternates until no more tokens can be placed.

The player who reaches or passes 100 wins the game.

Try the game without a chart. Can you keep track of the numbers in your head?

Nim Variations

When mathematicians study a problem, they often try making small changes, just to see what will happen. Nim is a wonderful game for this sort of investigation.

Encourage your students to alter the rules and make their own Nim games.

For instance, allow players to add any whole number from one to twenty on each turn. The player who reaches the end of the chart wins the game.

Or maybe the player who reaches the end loses the game. How does that change your strategy?

Or start at the highest number and subtract until you reach zero. But on each turn, you can subtract anything up to double the number your opponent used last.

What rules will you invent?

When you create a version you really like, give your new game a name. Teach it to a friend. Or send me an email, if you'd like me to share your game on my blog so kids all around the world can play.[†]

FOR FURTHER PLAY: Ask your librarian for help to find Sherron Pfeiffer's delightful (out of print) workbook *Creating NIM Games*.

— 43 —

Spill the Beans

two or more players, any chart

You will need five dried beans and a can to shake them in. Players will probably want scratch paper for calculations.

[†] *LetsPlayMath@gmail.com*

On your turn, shake out the beans, spilling them onto the chart. Write down the numbers they land on.

If a bean bounces off the chart, it scores zero.

Add your five numbers together to find your score. On each turn, add your new numbers to your total score.

The first player to reach or pass 1,000 points wins the game.

Or set your own scoring target based on how long you want to play.

— 44 —

Euclid's Game

two players or two teams, chart optional

You can play by writing numbers on plain paper, but it's easier to keep track using a highlight marker (with ink you can see through) on a printed hundred chart.

The first player picks any whole number from one to one hundred and writes that number on the paper (or marks that square on the hundred chart).

The second player writes or marks any other number, except that the second number may not be exactly double or exactly half the first choice.

On each succeeding turn, players subtract any two marked numbers to find and write a difference that has not yet been taken.

Play alternates until no more numbers can be made.

The player who marks the last number wins the game.

VARIATION: What happens if you omit the rule about the second number? Try playing Euclid's Game where the second number *may* be half or double the first one. Would you rather take your turn first or second?

— 44.5 —

Euclid's Challenge

Play several rounds of Euclid's Game on printed hundred charts. Circle the original pair of numbers in each game and use a highlighter to mark all the numbers you use.

Then study your collection of finished game boards.

Do you notice any patterns in the numbers marked on each game board?

Can you explain why some games have few numbers marked while others have many?

If you knew the first two numbers, would you be able to predict how many squares would be marked in the end?

CHAPTER 5

Multiplication and Factors

I used to think my job was
to teach students to see what I see.
I no longer believe this.

My job is to teach students to see;
and to recognize that no matter what the problem is,
we don't all see things the same way.

But when we examine our different ways of seeing,
and look for the relationships involved,
everyone sees more clearly;
everyone understands more deeply.

—RUTH PARKER

Making Sense of Multiplication

MULTIPLICATION IS THE GROUNDWORK FOR building an understanding of many topics in middle school and upper-level math, including fractions, ratios, and algebraic proportions.

As you continue to play with numbers and their relationships, introduce your child to ideas like oddness, evenness, balance, equal groups, equal parts, sharing, splitting, and the ratio word "per" (as in "buns per package" or "cookies per child").

And you can mix a few math words into your vocabulary, too. For instance, the *product* is the answer when you multiply two or more numbers. The *quotient* is the answer when you divide one number by another. When you try to split a number fairly, but it doesn't come out even, we call the leftovers the *remainder*.

— 45 —

Skip-Counting

Skip-counting stretches a child's mental addition skills beyond the standard math facts. It's a natural preparation for multiplication.

Skip count by twos or threes or tens, starting at any number. Begin by whisper counting: *one, two,* THREE, *four, five,* SIX … Let your finger run along the rows of the chart as you count, to keep track.

As children master skip-counting, they will no longer need to whisper the in-between numbers.

Remember to take turns. If you tell your daughter to count by fives, she gets to make you do elevens.

— 45.5 —

Color the Patterns

Look more closely at the skip-counting patterns. Colored Bingo disks are good for this because you can see the numbers through the translucent plastic. Or print several charts to color with pencils or felt-tip markers.

If you have my free *Hundred Charts Galore!* printables file, you can use the multi-chart pages to see more patterns at a glance.[†]

Show the numbers you hit when you count by twos. What pattern do they make?

Mark the counting-by-three pattern.

Which squares do you hit when you count by sevens?

Why does the counting-by-five pattern go down the way it does?

Why do the nines move slantwise across the chart?

What does the counting-by-ones pattern look like?

— 46 —

Advanced Skip-Counting

Count by whatever number you want, but start at an unusual place.

Count by two, but start with thirty-seven.

Or count by five, starting at eighteen.

Or for a tougher challenge, practice your mental subtraction skills. Count down by the number of your choice.

---

† *tabletopacademy.net/free-printables*

Times Tables

Print a blank hundred chart to create a *times table*—a chart that shows all the basic multiplication math facts—for each child. Or draw a larger grid on poster board to make a times table that extends to whatever numbers you desire.

I've heard of a teacher who makes all his students create a 30 × 30 times table. He wants them to understand that multiplication goes beyond the basic math facts. And all that practice helps each child develop strong math skills.

Write the numbers one to ten along the top of the chart, above the squares, one number for each column. Also write one to ten beside the left-hand column of the chart, one number for each row. These numbers are the *factors* that your child is going to multiply.

Help your children fill in their charts by skip-counting each row. The first row gets the counting-by-ones pattern, the second row counting-by-twos, and so on.

Like magic, the counting-by patterns will appear in the columns, too. Isn't that cool? Count down each column to check that you've got all the numbers in their right places.

After you complete your times table, the number in each square will be the product of that square's column and row numbers.

Have each child use a highlighter to color the multiplication facts they know by heart. As they learn additional facts, they can highlight more squares to track their progress in mastering multiplication.

Together, look for patterns on the times table.

What do you notice?

Sometimes, the same product shows up in more than one square. How many of these can you find?

Do any numbers appear in more than two squares?

Can you find the square numbers? A *square number* is a number that, if you have that many blocks, you can arrange them in rows and columns to make an exact square shape. One row with one block. Two rows with two blocks in each row. Three rows of three, and so on. Where are these numbers hiding on your times table?

Look at the numbers that are diagonal to the square numbers, touching at the corner. For example, 7 × 9 = 63 is diagonal to the square number 8 × 8 = 64. Many people call these the "near neighbor" products. Can you guess why? What pattern do you see in these numbers?

What if you follow the diagonals farther away from the squares? There's an interesting pattern in those numbers. Can you see it?

Play games with the multiplication facts. How would you modify the pattern games Connect Four (#26) or Battleship (#27) to work on a times table?

TEACHER'S TIP: I'm using the term "times table" to refer to the whole multiplication chart. But some people call each counting-by pattern the "times table" for that number and use the plural "times tables" to mean a single, complete chart. Either usage is fine, so go with what feels natural to you.

— 47.5 —

Scrambled Times Tables

A scrambled times table is just like a regular times table, except the numbers at the top and along the side are all mixed up.

Print a blank hundred chart, and write the numbers one to ten along the top and down the left-hand side, as above. But don't write the numbers in counting order. Mix them up. Can your child fill in the products on the scrambled chart?

Be sure to let your child scramble a chart for you to solve, too.

For a more advanced puzzle, instead of writing numbers at the top and side of your chart, just write in several of the products. To solve

X										
					4					
				1						
									100	
							49			
		64								
	36									
		25								
				16						
		81								

X										
								27		
									18	
								63		
									6	
								9		
									27	
								45		
	50		20		10		60			
		56		64		32				

Two puzzles from Iva Sallay's blog. Can you put the numbers 1–10 along the top and side of each times table so that the products shown make sense? Then fill in the rest of each chart.

this puzzle, your child must use those clues to decide where the scrambled factors go before he or she can fill in the rest of the chart.

FOR FURTHER PLAY: In addition to making your own scrambled times tables for each other to solve, you may enjoy Iva Sallay's blog Find the Factors. She offers a wide variety of puzzles rated from easy (level one) to challenging (level six), many with fun themes to encourage play.[†]

— 48 —

Times Tables on a Hundred Chart

Compare a hundred chart with a times table. Which numbers show up on both charts?

Color the hundred chart based on how often the numbers appear as answers on the times table. Pick a color for the numbers that appear zero times, another color for those that show up once, another for twice, and so on.

Look for patterns in your colored squares.

What do you notice? What do you wonder?

---

† *findthefactors.com*

Factors and Multiples

— 49 —

Factor Patterns

Look for factors and multiples on the hundred chart. *Factors* are the numbers that you multiply to get a product. And that product is the *multiple* of its factors.

Mark the times-table patterns (except the times-one pattern) by putting color-coded dots along one edge or corner of each square of a printed hundred chart. That is, all the multiples of two get a yellow dot, for instance, and the multiples of three get red dots, and so on.

Which numbers have the most dots — that is, have the most factors?

Which numbers have just one dot? What is special about those numbers?

Which numbers don't get any dots?

— 50 —

Common Multiples

When you explore the factor patterns, you will find many numbers that get more than one dot. These numbers are called *common multiples* of their factors. For example, six is a common multiple of two and three.

Look for patterns in the common multiples. On a printed chart, mark every multiple of two with a large "×" and every multiple of three with a large "+" sign. Which numbers end up marked by an asterisk? These are the common multiples of two and three. What do you notice about these numbers?

On another chart, use × and + to mark the multiples of three and four. What do you notice about their common multiples?

Try other combinations and see what patterns you can find. What are the common multiples of two and seven? Of four and eight? Six and nine?

What happens if you combine more than two numbers? Go back to the chart with multiples of two and three. Now mark every multiple of five with a large circle. What are the common multiples of two, three, and five?

MATH TIDBIT: In math, the word *common* usually means "shared." In addition to common multiples, mathematicians talk about common factors: the numbers six and nine share a common factor of three. Or you may have heard of fractions having common denominators, which means two (or more) fractions with the same number in their bottom parts.

— 51 —

Sieve of Eratosthenes

The ancient Greek scientist Eratosthenes was the first person to calculate accurately the earth's circumference. In 236 BC, he became the chief librarian of the Great Library of Alexandria, the capital of Ptolemaic Egypt.

In math, we remember Eratosthenes for his sieve, which is not a strainer for noodles and veggies. The Sieve of Eratosthenes is a quick way to filter out the primes from a list of numbers arranged in increasing order.

A *prime number* is a positive, whole number which has no factors smaller than itself except the number one (which is, of course, a factor of every whole number). Numbers that do have smaller factors are called *composite*.

1	2	3	4	5	6	7	8	9	10
11	12	13	14	15	16	17	18	19	20
21	22	23	24	25	26	27	28	29	30
31	32	33	34	35	36	37	38	39	40
41	42	43	44	45	46	47	48	49	50
51	52	53	54	55	56	57	58	59	60
61	62	63	64	65	66	67	68	69	70
71	72	73	74	75	76	77	78	79	80
81	82	83	84	85	86	87	88	89	90
91	92	93	94	95	96	97	98	99	100

The next prime number is seven. Some of its multiples have already been crossed out because they are also multiples of two, three, or five. Now you need to eliminate any that remain.

On a printed chart, shade in the box for the number one. One does not count as either prime or composite.

Circle the next unmarked number (two), and then cross out all of its multiples—that is, count by two and cross out every number you land on, except for two itself.

Circle the next unmarked number (three) and then cross out all of its multiples.

Continue circling unmarked numbers and crossing out their multiples until every number is either circled (prime) or crossed out (composite).

— 51.5 —

Math Humor

Go read the multitude of jokes about how "All odd numbers are prime."[†]

---

† *gdargaud.net/Humor/OddPrime.html*

— 52 —

Number Pattern Puzzles

Download Stuart Kay's "Blank 100 Grid Number Investigations" lesson (free registration required).[†]

The patterns relate to factors, multiples, prime numbers, and more. A few of the patterns involve simple algebra.

Challenge your students to deduce the secret behind each pattern of shaded squares.

Then have them make up pattern puzzles to match secret rules of their own.

Can you solve each other's puzzles?

— 53 —

Ulam's Spiral

Did you wonder about the spiral number charts in the *Hundred Charts Galore!* printables file? Print several copies and start exploring.

In 1963, mathematician Stanislaw Ulam got bored during a meeting, so he began to doodle. He wrote numbers spiraling around his paper, and then he started marking the primes. He noticed an interesting pattern. Several of the prime numbers grouped together to form diagonal lines.

Try it for yourself. On a spiral hundred chart, color each prime number square and connect them with lines. How many prime diagonals can you find?

Can you think of any reason why the prime numbers would tend to make diagonal patterns?

---

† *tes.com/teaching-resource/blank-100-grid-number-investigations-6340939*

100	99	98	97	96	95	94	93	92	91
65	64	63	62	61	60	59	58	57	90
66	37	36	35	34	33	32	31	56	89
67	38	17	16	15	14	13	30	55	88
68	39	18	5	4	3	12	29	54	87
69	40	19	6	1	2	11	28	53	86
70	41	20	7	8	9	10	27	52	85
71	42	21	22	23	24	25	26	51	84
72	43	44	45	46	47	48	49	50	83
73	74	75	76	77	78	79	80	81	82

The prime diagonals on a hundred chart. What other patterns can you find on a spiral hundred chart?

Try coloring other number patterns, like the skip-counting patterns, or square numbers, or Fibonacci numbers. What do those numbers look like on a spiral chart?

What happens if you make a different type of chart? Ulam's spiral turns tightly to make a squarish shape. But you could experiment with other spiral shapes on graph paper.

Try going several squares in one direction before the first turn, to make an oblong spiral.

Or leave a few squares blank in the middle, for a donut-shaped spiral.

How do the number patterns look on your new spiral charts?

TEACHER'S TIP: If you're puzzled about why the prime numbers tend to cluster along diagonal lines, it may help to identify the numbers that can't possibly be primes. Color in the even numbers on a spiral chart. Color the multiples of three, and the multiples of five. What do you notice about the squares that are left?

FOR FURTHER PLAY: Educator Megan Schmidt has enjoyed playing with spirals for years. A few summers back, she had the chance to share the fun with kids as a visiting math artist at the Minnesota State Fair. You can read the story at her blog and download a template for spiraling numbers far beyond the hundred chart.[†]

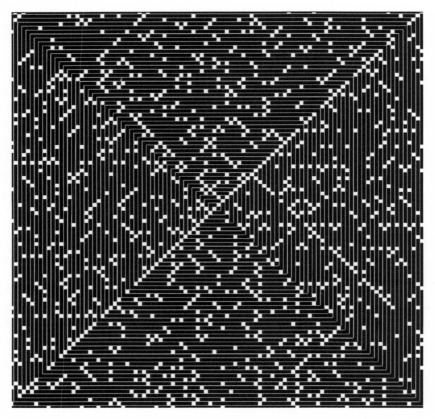

Your number spiral doesn't have to start with the number one.
If you start a Ulam spiral with forty-one, you get
an especially impressive prime diagonal.
The black squares are composite numbers, and the white are prime.

---

†   *mathybeagle.com/2016/08/26/spiraling-math-on-a-stick*
mathybeagle.com/2017/12/12/spiraling-the-hundred-chart-and-beyond

Multiplication Games

—54—

How Close to 100?

two or three players, printed chart

Print a blank hundred chart. You will also need two dice and a pencil or marker.

The goal of this cooperative game is to color in all the squares on the hundred chart.

On your turn, roll the dice. Color a rectangle with sides that match the numbers rolled.

For example, if you rolled a two and a four, you might color a rectangle with two rows and four squares in each row. Or you could make it four rows tall with two squares in each row. Can you see how either rectangle shows the product 2 × 4?

Can you explain why we say, "To find the area of a rectangle, multiply the length times the width"?

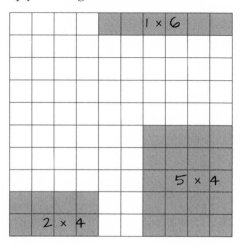

You rolled a three and a five, so you need to color a 3 × 5 rectangle. Where's the best place to squeeze it in?

If you can't fit your rectangle anywhere on the chart, you have to pass.

The game ends when all players have rolled the dice without being able to color a rectangle.

How close can you get to coloring the whole game board?

— 54.5 —

Rectangle Face-Off

two or more players, printed charts

Play as above, but players each color rectangles on their own printed chart. Whoever gets closest to filling all their squares wins the game.

— 55 —

Odd–Even–Prime Race

two or more players, any chart

You will also need a small toy or token for each player. All players begin at square one.

On your turn, roll two dice. You may choose to add or subtract these numbers to find how many squares you can move. The direction you move depends on the number you're starting from, as follows:

- ♦ If your token is starting on an odd number, move forward.

- ♦ From an even number (except two), move backward—but never lower than the first square.

- ♦ If you are starting on a prime number (including two), you may choose to either add, subtract, *or multiply* the dice. Move forward.

Two or more players may land on the same square.

The first person to reach or pass one hundred (or the highest number on your number chart) wins the game.

Teacher's Tip: This game was invented by teacher Ali Adams as a variation on more traditional number race games like #41 Race to 100. How would you change the rules to make up your own game?

— 56 —

Factors and Multiples

two players or two teams, printed chart

The first player marks an *even number less than fifty* on the hundred chart. Color in the square or just circle the number.

The second player marks any factor or multiple of that number.

For example, imagine the first player marked square forty-eight. Then the second player could mark two, four, twelve, sixteen, or any other factor of forty-eight. Or they could mark ninety-six, which is the only multiple of forty-eight on the chart.

Now imagine the second player chose to mark the number two. Then the first player could mark the number one, which is the only remaining factor of two. Or they could mark any even number (except forty-eight, which is already taken) because they are all multiples of two.

Players alternate, each time marking a new factor or multiple of the previous number played. You cannot mark a number square that has already been used.

The player who marks the last factor or multiple, leaving the opponent with no move, wins the game.

— 56.5 —

Factors and Multiples Solitaire

solitaire, chart optional

Try to find the longest possible chain of factors and multiples, according to the game rules above. Mark them on a printed chart, or just write a list on paper.

Keep track of the order in which you mark the numbers.

What do you notice?

Does it make you wonder?

Can you find a way to mark fifty or more numbers without breaking the chain?

Is it possible to use all the numbers on the hundred chart in one chain? Why not?

— 57 —

Tax Collector

two or more players, printed chart

You will need a printed chart, pencils or felt-tip markers, and scratch paper for keeping score.

One player is the tax collector, and all the others work together as a team of shop owners.

Each shop owner in turn marks (by drawing an X or coloring the square) any available number on the hundred chart. Add this number to the team's running total profit.

After each shop owner's turn, the tax collector marks all the factors of that number (which have not been previously marked) as tax. The tax collector adds these numbers to his or her running total.

The game continues with shop owners claiming a profit amount and the tax collector looking for factors to tax. Once a number has been marked by any player, it cannot be used again.

The game ends when the shop owners have no legal play.

Whoever collects the most money (profit or tax) wins.

WARNING: You must always pay the tax collector! No shop owner may mark a number that doesn't have any factors remaining. If you try to claim a number with no factors, the tax collector will take that whole amount as a penalty.

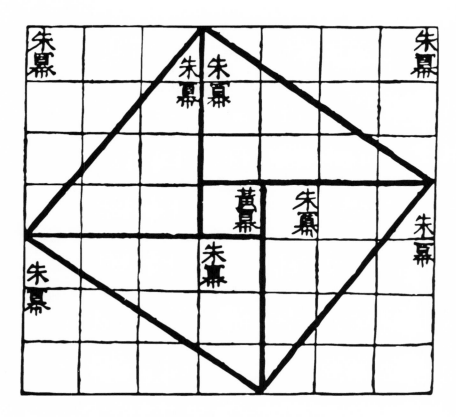

Chinese mathematicians of the Zhou dynasty used
a not-quite-100 grid to demonstrate the Pythagorean Theorem,
centuries before Pythagoras was born.

CHAPTER 6

Advanced Topics

At heart, mathematical thinking
is little more than
formalized common sense.

It always has been.

Which means it is something
we can all do.

—KEITH DEVLIN

Fractions, Decimals, and Percents

THE HUNDRED CHART CAN ALSO help your child understand fractions and learn to compare and convert between fractions, decimals, and percentages.

IMPORTANT NOTE: For most of these activities, you must use the 1–100 version of the hundred chart. The 0–99 version will not work, because you can't have a square of the chart that's worth zero percent or zero hundredths. The square is an actual something, but zero percent is nothing.

— 58 —

Fraction Strips

Print a few blank 120 charts and turn them sideways, in landscape orientation, so each chart has ten rows with twelve squares in each row. Cut out the rows to make fraction strips with twelve squares on each strip.

Color a different set of squares on each strip. On some fraction strips, arrange the colored squares all together at one end. On other strips, mix them around.

If we count each strip as one whole thing, what fraction of its squares is colored?

Match the strips that represent the same fraction.

On many of the strips, there will be more than one way to name the fraction. For example, if six squares are colored, we might call that $\frac{6}{12}$ or $\frac{3}{4}$ or $\frac{1}{2}$ of the strip. These alternate names are easiest to see when the colored squares are all at one end of the strip, because you can fold the strip to show the halves or fourths.

How many different fraction names can you find for each set of colored squares?

Complex Fractions

We could also call the strip with six colored squares "1½ thirds" of the whole strip. Can you show by folding why that name makes sense?

Or we might call the strip with five colored squares "2½ sixths."

When there is a fraction within a fraction like this, we call it a *complex fraction*, because it is more complicated than a *common* (or simple) fraction.

A complex fraction is like a puzzle, challenging us to find its secret identity—the common fraction that names the same amount of stuff.

For example, how much is 3⅓ fourths? One-fourth would be three of the twelve squares on a fraction strip. So three-fourths would be three sets of those three squares, or nine squares. Then we need to add one-third of the final fourth, which is one of the remaining three squares. So 3⅓ fourths must be ten squares in all.

$$3⅓ \text{ fourths} = \frac{10}{12} = \frac{5}{6}$$

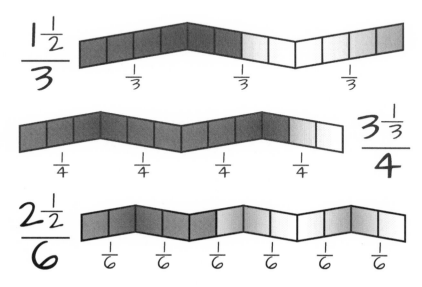

Complex fractions have other fractions inside them.

How many complex fractions can you find in your set of fraction strips?

CHALLENGE PUZZLES: Sometimes a complex fraction has a fraction or mixed number in its denominator. How can we make sense of that?

Can you figure out how much a one-and-a-halfth would be?

Remember, the denominator of a fraction tells you how many pieces of that size will make one whole unit.

So with our mystery fraction, it takes one and one-half pieces to make a complete fraction strip. What size would one piece be?

Experiment by folding a fraction strip into one longer section plus a smaller part that is half its size. The longer section is the one-and-a-halfth piece.

It takes one and one-half pieces to make one whole strip.

A one-and-a-halfth is a useful fraction. It was a favorite of the ancient Egyptian scribes, who used it to solve all sorts of practical math problems.

Egyptians thought of fractions as single pieces like a third or a fifth. We call these *unit fractions* and write them with a numerator of one: ⅓ or ⅕. But Egyptians didn't bother with numerators.

For example, the amount we call "three-fourths" the Egyptians thought of as "a half and a fourth."

Little pieces were a nuisance to work with, so they wanted to cut the largest pieces they could. That's why they loved using a one-and-a-halfth.

Let's try another puzzle. How about a one-and-a-thirdth? How many of those pieces make a whole strip? Can you fold a strip into one

Can you find the number "one and a half" hiding in the Egyptian hieroglyph?

large section plus a smaller part that's one-third as big? What simple fraction names the larger section of that strip?

Or how much would a two-thirdth be? In that case, it only takes two-thirds of a piece to make a complete strip, so the whole piece must be greater than one. A two-thirdth's secret identity is a mixed number. Can you unmask it?

Make up some challenge fraction mysteries of your own.

TEACHER'S TIP: Yes, there are answers at the end of the book. But don't peek—fidget with your fraction strips and try to work these out. A puzzle is no fun when someone gives it away.

— 59 —

Fractions of One Hundred

Look for common fractions on the hundred chart. Trim the margins off a printed chart, so you can fold it to show the fractional parts. Or mark the fraction with your finger, running it across the squares.

What number is half of one hundred? Can you show on the chart why that's true? If you run your finger across half of the chart, which number do you stop at?

What number is three-fourths of one hundred? How can you prove it? What other fractions of one hundred can you show by folding or by running your finger along the squares? One-tenth? Two-fifths?

Can you find some complex fractions of one hundred? For instance, how far would you run your finger to touch "1⅕ fourths" of the chart? Let's see: one-fourth of one hundred would be twenty-five squares. And one-fifth of twenty-five would add five more squares. So "1⅕ fourths" must be thirty squares in all.

Take turns naming fractions of one hundred for the other person to show on the chart.

Can you find a number that is one-third of 100?

— 59.5 —

Equivalent Fractions of One Hundred

Fifty squares of a hundred chart make the fraction fifty-hundredths. That same amount can also be named one-half because fifty squares cover half of the hundred chart.

Fractions can have many names, like a secret agent with many alias identities.

Can you find another name for one-half on the hundred chart?

For example, there are ten rows on the chart, which means each row is one-tenth of the chart. Five rows would be $\frac{5}{10}$ of the whole chart. So five-tenths is another alias for one-half.

Or try a complex fraction. Two entire rows are one-fifth of the whole chart. Four rows are two-fifths. Would it make sense to call five rows "2½ fifths" of the chart? That means "2½ fifths" is another alias for one-half.

When two different fractions name the same amount of stuff, we call them *equivalent fractions*.

Take turns finding equivalent fractions on the hundred chart. One person names a fraction, and the other tries to find an alias identity for it.

— 60 —

Fractions of a Fraction

Fifty squares cover one-half of the hundred chart. How many squares are one-half of one-half of the chart? What fraction names that part of the whole chart?

How many squares are six-tenths of the chart? Now what would be one-third of that six-tenths? What fraction names that amount?

Can you name other fractions of fractions? Show the squares on your hundred chart, and then find the fraction name for the same amount.

When we say "two groups of three," we are talking about multiplication. We can write it in symbols this way:

$$2 \times 3 = 6$$

Likewise, we can write "one-half of three-fifths" as multiplication like this:

$$\tfrac{1}{2} \times \tfrac{3}{5} = ?$$

Since one-fifth of the hundred chart is two rows or twenty squares, three-fifths of the chart must be three times as much: six rows or sixty squares. How much is half of that? We can solve the multiplication puzzle this way (and throw in a couple of equivalent fractions):

$$\tfrac{1}{2} \times \tfrac{3}{5} = \tfrac{30}{100}$$

$$= 1\tfrac{1}{2} \text{ fifths} = \tfrac{3}{10}$$

Notice that multiplication doesn't always make a bigger number than what you started with. If you multiply by a fraction that is less than one, your answer will only be that fractional part of your original number.

Make up fraction-of-a-fraction puzzles for each other to solve.

— 61 —

Convert Numbers: Decimals

If we say that the hundred chart is one whole unit, then what part is each row (in decimal notation)? If you run your finger along one row, how much of the chart have you touched?

There are ten rows, so each row is 0.1 of the whole chart.

What is the value of each square?

There are one hundred squares. Each square is 0.01 of the whole chart.

Can you color 0.47 of the chart? Or show it by running your finger along the squares.

What decimal would mean the same as one-fifth of the chart?

Take turns naming fractions for the other person to convert to decimal numbers, or decimals for them to convert to fractions.

— 62 —

Multiply Decimals

Notice the rows and columns of your hundred chart. Can you see that one row is one-tenth of the whole chart? That one column is also one-tenth of the chart? And that one square is one-tenth of a row (or column)?

We can use these tenths relationships to explore what it means to multiply decimals.

TEACHER's TIP 1: First, review the rectangular model of multiplication. (Do you remember #54 How Close to 100?) In a rectangle, you can multiply the number of rows by the number of things in each row to find out the whole amount. For example, to show the product 5×7, you might color a rectangle with five rows and seven squares in each row. Or you could make it seven rows tall with five squares in each row.

We can multiply decimals on the hundred chart using rectangles, too. We just need to count our rows and columns in decimal parts.

The first decimal factor in our calculation tells how many rows we need in our rectangle. If the first factor is 0.1, we need one row because that's one-tenth of the whole chart. For 0.7 we would use seven rows.

The second factor tells how many squares to include in each row. Each square is one-tenth of the row. So if we are multiplying by 0.4, we need four-tenths of each row, which is four squares.

MATH TIDBIT: Remember that multiplication is *commutative*, which means it works in any order. If it makes sense for you to think of the second factor as the number of rows and the first factor as how many squares per row, that's perfectly fine. Or think of one factor as columns and the other as rows per column—you'll still get the right size rectangle.

Let's try a decimal multiplication puzzle:

$$0.3 \times 0.8 = ?$$

The first factor is 0.3, so we need three rows to make our rectangle. Three-tenths of the whole hundred chart.

The second factor is 0.8, so we need eight-tenths of each row. That means our rectangle will go over eight squares.

Color in this rectangle on your hundred chart, or run your finger along the squares. Three rows with eight squares in each row is twenty-four squares in all. And what part of the whole chart is that? Each square is one hundredth of the chart. What decimal number represents twenty-four hundredths?

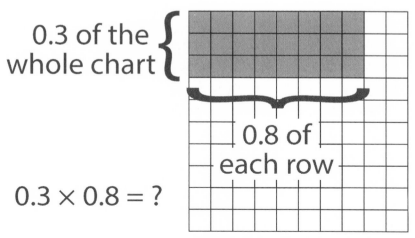

If your hundred chart counts as one whole thing, then each row is one-tenth. And each square is one-tenth of a row.

So we can write:

$$0.3 \times 0.8 = 0.24$$

Take turns naming decimal multiplication puzzles for the other person to solve by showing the rectangle.

This method of multiplying decimals will help your child avoid a common mistake many students make. Consider the following comparison between addition and multiplication:

$$0.2 + 0.3 = 0.5$$
So can we say that
$$0.2 \times 0.3 = 0.6?$$
No!
But why not?

Run your finger across a rectangle with two rows and three squares in each row. That is two-tenths of three-tenths of the hundred chart. How many squares in all? And how much is that of the whole chart?

With only six squares, the rectangle is tiny, isn't it? Each square is one hundredth of the chart. So our product is six hundredths:

$$0.2 \times 0.3 = 0.06$$

Teacher's Tip 2: Avoid giving your children a rule about counting decimal places. Instead, help them think about *what the numbers mean*. A decimal times another decimal is like taking a fraction of a fraction—you get something really small. The rule can come later, after your kids build a foundation of understanding.

Can you figure out how to make a rectangle for a multiplication that includes more than just tenths? How would you show this decimal multiplication puzzle:

$$0.4 \times 0.65 = ?$$

You need four rows to represent four-tenths of the chart. And 0.65 is midway between 0.6 and 0.7, so you need six and one-half squares in each row of your rectangle. How many squares in all? And what part is that of the whole chart?

We can add the squares and half-squares together to find the size of our rectangle:

$$0.4 \times 0.65 = 0.26$$

The rectangular model of multiplication works, even when the dimensions of your rectangle are not full squares.

— 63 —

Convert Numbers: Percents

Can you see the two zeros of "100" in the percent symbol "%"? *Percent* means "per hundred." Or you could say "out of every hundred."

When we look at the chart by rows and squares, we can say that:

100% of 100 = 100 squares
10% of 100 = 1 row = 10 squares
1% of 100 = 1 square

So 30% means "thirty per hundred" or "thirty out of every hundred." Can you show that much on the hundred chart?

Can you show 75% of the chart? 90%? 23%?

Find and name other percents on the chart. What is the decimal name for that amount? What is the fraction name?

— 63.5 —

Percents of Other Values

What would happen if the whole chart were worth some number other than one hundred?

Each row would still be one-tenth or ten percent of the chart's total value. And each square would be one-hundredth or one percent.

For example, what if the whole chart counts from one to eight hundred? How much would one row be worth? Or one square?

$$100\% \text{ of } 800 = 800$$
$$10\% \text{ of } 800 = 80$$
$$1\% \text{ of } 800 = 8$$

So each square would be worth eight of whatever we are counting.

Or what if the chart was worth less than one hundred? If the whole chart is worth sixty, what is the value of one row? Or one square?

$$100\% \text{ of } 60 = 60$$
$$10\% \text{ of } 60 = 6$$
$$1\% \text{ of } 60 = ?$$

Remember, one square is always worth one-tenth of a row. So if one row is worth six, then:

$$1\% \text{ of } 60 = \tfrac{1}{10} \text{ of } 6$$
$$= \tfrac{6}{10} = 0.6$$

MATH TIDBIT: Percent values that are relatively easy to calculate in your head are called *benchmark percents*. You can put them together to figure out more difficult amounts or to make estimates. Here are some common benchmark values:

- ◆ 100% = the whole amount
- ◆ 50% = half of the amount
- ◆ 25% = one-fourth of the amount, or half of one-half
- ◆ 10% = one-tenth of the whole amount
- ◆ 1% = one-tenth of 10%, or a tenth of one-tenth of the whole amount

So how could we figure out what is 23% of 900? Imagine that the whole chart is worth 900, so a tenth of that is ninety, and one percent is nine. How much is twenty-three percent?

$$100\% \text{ of } 900 = 900$$
$$10\% \text{ of } 900 = 90$$
$$1\% \text{ of } 900 = 9$$
$$20\% \text{ of } 900 = 2 \times 10\% \text{ of } 900 = 180$$
$$3\% \text{ of } 900 = 3 \times 1\% \text{ of } 900 = 27$$
$$23\% \text{ of } 900 = 180 + 27 = 207$$

What if we don't know the value of the whole chart, but we do know part of it? If 8% of the total is 240, how much would 100% be worth?

$$8\% \text{ of "?"} = 240$$
$$1\% \text{ of "?"} = 240 \div 8 = 30$$
$$100\% \text{ of "?"} = 100 \times 30 = 3{,}000$$

So the whole chart must be worth three thousand. Wow!

Make percent puzzles for each other to solve: "If the whole chart is worth _____, what is the value of _____% of it?"

Or "If _____% of the hundred chart is worth _____, how much is the whole chart?"

— 64 —

Math Mosaics

Gather several sheets of paper in different colors. Cut them into squares that fit a blank hundred chart.

Glue paper squares to the chart to make any pattern or design you like. Or arrange them randomly if you prefer.

Can you figure out all the following data for your chart?

- ◆ What fraction of the picture is each color?
- ◆ What percent of the design is that?
- ◆ If the whole chart counts as "one," what decimal part is covered by each color?

Do all your color fractions add up to one? Do the decimals for your colors sum to one? What is the total of your color percents?

— 64.5 —

Op Art

Op Art is a geometric art style that was popular in the 1960s. Artists used colored shapes (like the Math Mosaics above) or black and white to make optical illusion patterns that seemed to move on the canvas.

Look up some Op Art paintings online.

Which ones do you like best? Can you figure out how the artists created their illusions?

You can create your own Op Art drawing similar to Bridget Riley's 1961 painting "Movement in Squares."

Follow these steps:

♦ Print a blank hundred or 120 chart.

♦ Use a ruler to draw vertical lines that cut some columns into halves, thirds, and smaller bits.

♦ Then color your drawing like a checkerboard.

Do your squares seem to bend into the paper?

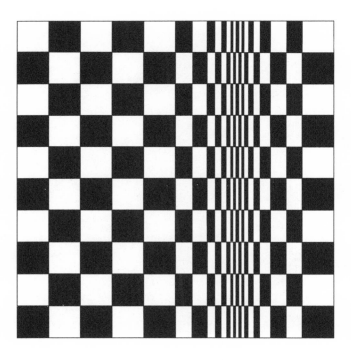

The more lines you make, getting ever thinner, the more the illusion will seem to sink into your paper.

Probability, Strategy, and Logic

— 65 —

Random Walk Game

2–4 players, deck of cards, any chart

Each player will need a distinct token, such as a small toy dinosaur or crumpled ball of colored paper. Place each token in a square near the middle of the chart. Tokens may not share a square.

Remove the tens and face cards from the deck. Spread the remaining cards face down to make a fishing pond.

On your turn, draw one card from the pond.

Imagine the squares around your token numbered like a phone pad, as if your token was sitting on the number five. That means two is directly above you, toward the top of the chart, eight is down below, four and six to your left and right. The odd numbers are on the diagonals from your position.

If you draw a five, leave your token where it is. Otherwise, move one square in the direction indicated by the number on your card. But if another player's token is already on that square, you may not move.

Mix your card back into the fishing pond at the end of your turn. Shuffle the whole pond, so no one can tell which card you drew.

The first player to move off the chart wins the game.

What did you notice about the way your token moved along the board? After you left your starting square, did you ever return to it?

Did every player move toward the edge of the board at the same average speed?

What if you played on a chart with one million squares instead of one hundred? Would anyone ever reach the edge of the chart?

1	2	3	4	5	6	7	8	9	10
11	12	13	14	15	16	17	18	19	20
21	22	23	24	25	1	2	3	29	30
31	32	33	34	35	4	5	6	39	40
41	42	43	44	45	7	8	9	49	50
51	52	53	54	55	56	57	58	59	60
61	62	63	64	65	66	67	68	69	70
71	72	73	74	75	76	77	78	79	80
81	82	83	84	85	86	87	88	89	90
91	92	93	94	95	96	97	98	99	100

Imagine your current position covered by a phone keypad. For a token on square 37, the keypad would look like this.

— 65.5 —

Real-World Random Walks

Many real-life situations can be modeled as a random walk—for example, the fluctuation of stock prices, the Brownian motion of a particle on the surface of a pond, or the money in a gambler's pocket. Google uses random walks to decide which web pages best match your search term, and Twitter uses a random walk to generate suggestions of people you might like to follow.

The best way to understand the mathematics of a random walk is to begin with a limited scenario. Imagine that you can only move along a single line, forward or backward. Flip a coin or roll a die. If you flip heads or roll an odd number, take one step forward. If you flip tails or roll an even number, step backward.

What is the probability that you will move forward? Backward? What are the chances that you'll return to your starting position? How far away from your starting position do you expect you will go?

For Further Play: The National Museum of Mathematics offers a classroom lesson to help students understand linear (on a single line) random walks.[†]

If you know coding, can you think of a way to program a random walk? Check out this investigation by Mike Lawler and sons:[‡]

— 66 —

Gomoku

two players, any chart

You can play on a blank or numbered chart. Players will each need a matching set of their own tokens, such as colored glass gems, black and white stones, or small, crumpled balls of colored paper. Or you can mark X and O on a printed chart.

Take turns marking any unclaimed square on the hundred chart.

The first player to form an unbroken five-in-a-row chain horizontally, vertically, or diagonally wins the game.

But if the player fails to notice his or her winning row before the next player marks a square, it doesn't count. Keep playing until someone makes a new row of five.

As in Tic-Tac-Toe, it's possible (though rare) for a hundred chart Gomoku game to end in a draw.

Optional Rule 1: Use a numbered chart. Players must make up a calculation that equals the number in the square they want to mark.

Optional Rule 2: A row of six is called an *overline* and does not win the game. You must have exactly five squares to win.

---

† *momath.org/wp-content/uploads/2016/11/Random-Walk-lesson-9.12.15.pdf*
‡ *mikesmathpage.wordpress.com/2016/06/19/an-introduction-to-random-walks-for-kids*
mikesmathpage.wordpress.com/2017/04/08/random-walks-with-kids

— 66.5 —

Computer Gomoku

one player vs. the computer

If you enjoy Gomoku, you can download a freeware version from the PC Gaming website. But it doesn't come with a hundred chart.[†]

— 67 —

Twenty Questions

two or more players, chart optional

Players may want a printed hundred chart to keep track of clues as they try to guess a number. If you are not using a chart, everyone should agree on the range of possible numbers before starting the game.

One player is "It"— the person with a secret everyone else is trying to guess. "It" chooses a secret number within the permissible range.

The other players take turns asking questions that can be answered with a simple "yes" or "no."

Questions might include the following:

- Is your number even?

- Is it less than sixty?

- Is your number prime?

- Is it divisible by five?

To add variety to the game, you may not repeat the same type of question too often. For example, if you ask whether the number is greater than some value, you must ask at least two different types of

---

[†] *pcgaming.ws/viewgame.php?game=gomoku*

questions before making another greater-than query.

If questions are deemed too similar, "It" may refuse to answer them. Unanswered questions do not count toward the limit of twenty.

If players have trouble thinking of questions, provide a list of math vocabulary: greater or less than, odd, even, digits, sum, difference, factor, multiple, divisible, prime, composite, square number, and so on.

When you think you know the answer, you may not simply shout it out. You must pose it as a specific question: "Is your number seventeen?"

The player who correctly guesses the number becomes "It" for the next round. But if no one solves the puzzle after twenty questions, the current "It" reveals the secret number and gets to choose a new one.

— 68 —

Number Riddles

two or more players, printed charts

Try teacher educator Terry Kawas's "Guess the Number" and "Hundred Board Logic" puzzles. Then make up similar puzzles of your own.[†]

To host your own number riddle game, decide on the range of numbers allowed and give each player a printed chart to help in writing their clues. Players work separately to create their riddle. Then everyone comes together for a riddling party.

Choose a secret number that the other players will try to guess. Write four or more clues about your number.

If I chose the number fifteen, for example, I might write the following clues:

♦ My number has two digits.

♦ The number is odd.

♦ My number is less than fifty.

---

† *mathwire.com/problemsolving/guessthenumber.pdf (PDF)*
mathwire.com/problemsolving/hblogic.pdf (PDF)

- It's a product of two prime numbers.

- The sum of the digits is six.

Arrange your number riddle clues in order from the hardest to the easiest. The hardest clue is the one that would apply to the most possible answers, like "My number has two digits."

Check your riddle on your printed chart by crossing off the numbers eliminated by each clue. Every clue must reduce the possible answers by at least one number. And there must be no other numbers that fit all your clues.

In testing my clues, I marked off all the numbers but fifteen and thirty-three. Oops! I can't allow two possible answers. So I need to add one more clue:

- You can make my number in change without using pennies.

When everyone is ready, it's time to play.

One player (the *riddler*) reads his or her clues aloud while the other players try to guess the secret number. The guessing players may want fresh printed hundred charts (or multi-chart pages from my *Hundred Charts Galore!* printables file) to keep track of the clues.

You may take one guess for each clue the riddler reads. If there is more than one person on the guessing team, they may all discuss each clue before the player whose turn it is makes a guess.

You can play for the simple fun of guessing.

Or keep score by counting how many clues you needed before you guessed correctly. With more than two players, track your score individually—but all the players of the guessing team get the same score for each number.

For example, imagine that Tom reads four clues before the team guesses his number. Everyone else will add four to their score. Tom doesn't add anything because he's the riddler. But when Janelle reads clues, Tom will be on the guessing team, so he will score points then.

After all the secret numbers have been guessed, the player with the lowest total score wins the game.

Charlie's Delightful Machine

one player or small group, online

Charlie's Delightful Machine is an interactive online puzzle for middle school and high school students.[†]

The machine has four colored lights, each controlled by a function rule.

- ◆ Level 1 rules are linear sequences of the form "$an + b$" with the numbers a and b between two and twelve.

- ◆ Level 2 rules are quadratic sequences of the form "$an^2 + bn + c$" with a limited to zero or one.

- ◆ Level 3 rules are quadratic sequences of the form "$an^2 + bn + c$" with $a = 0, 0.5, 1, 2$ or 3.

If you choose a number that satisfies the rule, the light will go on.

Use a printed hundred chart and four colored pencils or felt-tip markers to keep track of which lights glow when you choose a number.

Can you figure out the rules?

Can you find a number that makes all the lights come on?

Hit the "Restart" button to get a new set of rules.

---

† *nrich.maths.org/7024*

Have a Math Debate

THE POINT OF A MATH debate isn't that one answer is "right" while the other is "wrong." You may choose either side of the question. The important thing is how well you support your argument.

— 70 —

100 or 99?

Should the hundred chart count 1–100 or 0–99?

Does it feel more natural to start counting with zero or to start at one?

Children often think of zero as merely "nothing." Does having zero on the chart help them understand that it's a legitimate number?

Is it really a "hundred" chart if it doesn't have the number "100"?

Children often have trouble remembering which number comes after somethingty-nine. Does it help to see the next decade number on the same row (29 and then 30) as in the 1–100 chart?

Or is it more important for children to see all the numbers in a single decade (for instance, all the thirty-somethings) together in a single row, as in the 0–99 chart?

Give evidence for your opinion and critique each other's reasoning.

— 71 —

Count Up or Down?

Traditional hundred charts (either 0–99 or 1–100) start with the smaller numbers at the top and flow down toward the bottom like the days on a calendar. We read them line by line, just as we read the page of a book.

Bottoms-up charts rearrange the squares so that as we count to greater numbers, we climb higher on the board.

Which way makes intuitive sense to you?

Which chart do you think would best help young children learn about numbers?

— 72 —

Grid or Number Line?

Cut a printed number chart into rows and paste them into a long number line.

Which is easier to count on?

Which makes it easier to see number patterns?

Try playing the Race to 100 game (#41) or doing the Sieve of Eratosthenes (#51) on the number line. Is it easier when the numbers are in a straight line, or when they're on a grid?

Which do you prefer? Why?

— 73 —

Rounding Data

The standard elementary school rule is to round somethingty-five numbers up to the next multiple of ten.

This seems balanced because numbers ending in 0, 1, 2, 3, and 4 round down. Numbers ending in 5, 6, 7, 8, and 9 round up.

But the somethingty-zero numbers are already down. They simply remain themselves. So really, we are rounding four digits down (1, 2, 3, 4) but five digits up (5, 6, 7, 8, 9).

Could that throw our data off?

Some argue that when we apply the elementary rule to a large amount of data, it creates a distortion that makes the overall results seem too high.

So researchers may use a more complicated rule like "round to even." That is, if you are rounding a number midway between two values, you would round it to the even-numbered option. Theoretically, that makes you round up or down each half the time, keeping your data in balance.

Does using the elementary school rounding rule actually distort data?

How could we detect such a distortion?

Which rule do you prefer?

— 74 —

Adding Fractions

When you add fractions, you face a problem that most people never think of. Namely, you have to decide exactly what you are talking about.

For instance, what is one-tenth plus one-tenth?

Well, you might say that:

$\frac{1}{10}$ of one particular hundred chart
+ $\frac{1}{10}$ of the same chart
= $\frac{2}{10}$ of that hundred chart

But, you might also say that:

$\frac{1}{10}$ of one chart
+ $\frac{1}{10}$ of another chart
= $\frac{2}{20}$ of the *pair* of charts

That is, you started off counting on two independent charts. But when you put them together, you ended up with a double chart. Two hundred squares in all. Which made each row in the final set worth one-twentieth of the whole pair of charts.

So what happens if you see this question on a math test?

$$\tfrac{1}{10} + \tfrac{1}{10} = \,?$$

If you write the answer "$\tfrac{2}{20}$," you know the teacher will mark it wrong. Is that fair? Why, or why not?

Does the example with the hundred charts seem forced? Let's think instead about groups of friends. Three friends here, and three over there. Each group has two boys and a girl, so each girl is one-third of her group.

Now if the two groups come together for a pizza party, what fraction of this larger group is girls?

Would it make sense to write that situation like this:

$$\tfrac{1}{3} \text{ of one group}$$
$$+ \tfrac{1}{3} \text{ of the other group}$$
$$= \tfrac{2}{6} \text{ of the whole gang?}$$

Why, or why not?[†]

---

† *marilynburnsmathblog.com/can-1-3-1-3-2-6-it-seemed-so*

Mathematics is a process of constructing knowledge, not acquiring it. Children need to do what "real" mathematicians do—explore and invent for the rest of their lives.

—SUSAN OHANIAN

CONCLUSION

Two Problem-Solving Superpowers

IN HELPING OUR CHILDREN LEARN math, we must always remember the value of play.

Playfulness eliminates the performance anxiety many students feel with math worksheets and tests. Play encourages both children and parents to try new ideas and explore unfamiliar concepts.

When adults play along, we reinforce the value of mathematical activities. If the project or game is worthy of our attention, then it becomes more attractive to our children.

As we watch our kids' responses and listen to their comments during play, we discover how well they really understand math. Where do they get confused? What do they do when they're stuck? Can they use the number relationships they do remember to figure out something they don't know? How easily do they give up?

"Language should be part of the activity," says math teacher and author Claudia Zaslavsky. "Talk while you and your child are playing games. Ask questions that encourage your child to describe her actions and explain her conclusions."

Real education, learning that sticks for a lifetime, comes through person-to-person interactions. Our children absorb more from the give and take of discussion with an adult than from even the best workbook or teaching video.

As homeschooler Lucinda Leo explains, "My long-term goal is for my kids to be independent learners, but the best way for that to happen is for me to be by their side now, enjoying puzzles and stories, asking good questions and modeling creative problem-solving strategies."

Online Resources

Did you enjoyed the activities in this book? Are you ready for more mathy fun? Here are a few resources to keep you and your children playing with numbers, shapes, and logic.

After I sent this manuscript to the editor, I stumbled on two more ways to use a hundred chart. For young children, Dan Finkel's Math for Love blog has a delightful hundred chart game called, well, "The Hundred Chart Game." And for older students, check out MathPickle's area puzzle Blotch.[†]

You can bring mathematical play to the dinner table with ideas from John Stevens's free email newsletter Tabletalk Math.[‡]

Many real-life math situations involve counting, measurement, and estimation. Try the open-ended questions on John Stevens's Would You Rather? website.[§]

A hundred chart is like a number line cut into strips. So playing with number lines sounds like a natural next step to me. Explore Chris Shore's and Andrew Stadel's hands-on ideas for "clothesline math."[¶]

[†] *mathforlove.com/lesson/the-hundred-chart-game*
mathpickle.com/project/blotch
[‡] *tabletalkmath.com*
[§] *wouldyourathermath.com*
[¶] *clotheslinemath.com*
estimation180.com/clothesline.html

And if your children enjoy learning math through play, you might consider my other playful math books from Tabletop Academy Press.†

Your Child's Problem-Solving Superpowers

Learning math requires more than mastering number facts and memorizing rules. At its heart, math is a way of thinking. So more than anything else, we need to help our kids learn to think mathematically—to make sense of math problems and persevere in figuring them out.

Many students (and parents) struggle with math problems. They don't know where to start, and they doubt their ability to find the answer.

Fear becomes a mental brick wall.

But our children possess two problem-solving superpowers which can blast through that wall. We just need to help them recognize and use those powers.

The *Superpower of Observation* is our children's ability to see what is in front of them. They already have this power. They only need to slow down and pay attention.

That's why many of the hundred chart activities included questions like, "What do you notice? What do you see?"

You can help your children learn to see with mathematical eyes by taking turns making "I notice …" statements. Act as the scribe, writing down (without comment) everything you and your child see.

Noticing usually begins at the surface level. Children make obvious and often silly observations. But as we continue our list, both children and adults find our eyes opening to new facts and relationships within the topic—including the types of mathematical noticings that can help solve a problem.

The *Superpower of Speculation* is our children's natural curiosity about the world. We need to encourage our kids to be curious about math, too.

---

† *tabletopacademy.net/playful-math-books*

That's why many of the hundred chart activities included questions like, "What do you think? Does it make you wonder?"

You can help your children apply these questions to whatever math they are trying to learn.

After observing the details of a math topic or problem, make a new list of "I wonder …" statements. Again, take turns with your child, writing down all the wonderings without comment.

By writing down the things our children say, we create a safe environment for them to explore their thoughts without fear of grades or judgment. As author Max Ray-Riek points out in his book *Powerful Problem Solving*: "Everyone can notice something, and everyone has something they wonder about."

Whenever your children need to learn a new idea in math, or whenever they get stuck on a tough homework problem, return to the superpowers of observation and speculation. Take a few minutes to create "Things I Notice" and "Things I Wonder" lists.

Sometimes extend your observations and speculations beyond the immediate situation to help your child explore the awe and beauty in mathematical ideas. Ponder questions like, "Will numbers ever end? Is there anything bigger than infinity? Are there numbers between the squares on our hundred chart? How many fractions could we fit into the space between zero and one?"

For more tips on teaching students to brainstorm about math, check out these online resources from the Math Forum:

- Ever Wonder What They'd Notice? by Annie Fetter[†]
- Beginning to Problem Solve with "I Notice/I Wonder"[‡]
- Noticing and Wondering in High School[§]

Problem solving is a habit of mind that you and your children can learn and grow in. Help your kids practice slowing down and paying attention to understand fully a problem situation. Discover within

---

[†]   *youtu.be/a-Fth6sOaRA*
[‡]   *tinyurl.com/brainstorm-math (PDF)*
[§]   *tinyurl.com/maxray-noticing*

yourselves the superpowers of mathematical thinking.

… and may the Math be with you!

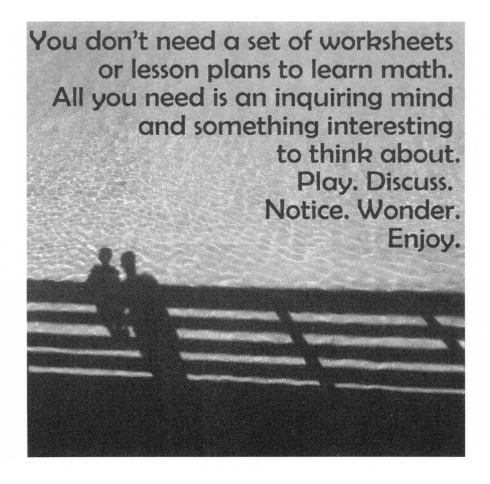

You don't need a set of worksheets or lesson plans to learn math. All you need is an inquiring mind and something interesting to think about. Play. Discuss. Notice. Wonder. Enjoy.

Answers to Selected Problems

Chapter 2: Counting

Make Change

If you are making change for a dollar, then you need enough coins to make any value from one to ninety-nine cents. That requires at least nine coins: four pennies, one nickel, two dimes, one quarter, and one half-dollar.

If you don't have a half-dollar coin, then you will need two additional quarters, for ten coins in all.

And if the coins in your country have different values, then you'll need enough of the smaller-denomination coins to make one less than each larger denomination. And enough coins total to make one less than your smallest paper bill.

Why do we need "one less" of each amount?

Making change is how a shopkeeper gives back the excess money when a customer buys something. If the customer didn't buy anything, there would be no need to make change. So we assume the item they bought costs at least one of our smallest-denomination coins.

Chapter 4: Addition and Subtraction

Next-Door Neighbors

Apartment-house neighbors are ten apart, numbers like 32 and 42. If someone tells you the sum, you can subtract that extra ten and then divide the result in half. That will give you the smaller of the two numbers—then add ten to get the larger number.

But numbers that sit diagonal to each other may be either nine or eleven apart. Since you don't know which way the diagonal slants, there is no way to discover them just from their sum.

Line Patterns

The line pattern sum for any line is the average of the numbers times the number of squares in the line. For odd-numbered lines, the middle number is the average.

Euclid's Challenge

The pattern of numbers on a finished game board is related to the greatest common divisor of the two original numbers. For more information, look up the Euclidean Algorithm.

Or read Rózsa Péter's delightful story about teaching the Euclidean Algorithm to a classroom of curious twelve-year-old girls.[†]

Chapter 5: Multiplication and Factors

Factors and Multiples Solitaire

The longest Factors and Multiples chain reported so far contains seventy-six numbers. Wow![‡]

Chapter 6: Advanced Topics

Complex Fractions

A one-and-one-halfth is another name for two-thirds.

A one-and-one-thirdth can be more simply named three-fourths.

A two-thirdth is more commonly known as three halves, or one and one-half.

In an Egyptian hieroglyph fraction, the number of tally marks under the oval tells the size of the fraction piece. If there were two marks, that would be the fraction "½." But in the hieroglyph for "⅔" they made one and a half tally marks.

[†]   denisegaskins.com/2018/08/15/mathematics-is-worthy
[‡]   nrich.maths.org/5468/solution

Random Walk Game

Mathematicians tell us that even on a million-chart game board, someone would eventually win, if you played long enough.

Personally, I would concede the game at the start.

Which is, incidentally, the reasoning behind the Gambler's Ruin. No matter how much money the gambler starts with or how much he wins, if he keeps placing bets, he will eventually reach the edge of his budget and go broke.

Quotes and Reference Links

ALL THE WEBSITE LINKS IN this book were checked before publication in November 2018, but the Internet is volatile. If a website disappears, you can run a browser search for the author's name or article title. Or try entering the web address at the Internet Archive Wayback Machine.
archive.org/web/web.php

ADAMS, ALI. "Pure Primes Game," Heliwave website, 2009.
heliwave.com/PurePrimes.pdf (PDF)

ANTONICK, GARY. "The Tax Collector," *The New York Times* Numberplay blog, April 13, 2015.
wordplay.blogs.nytimes.com/2015/04/13/finkel-4

AZAD, KALID. "Learning How to Count (Avoiding the Fencepost Problem)," Better Explained website.
betterexplained.com/articles/learning-how-to-count-avoiding-the-fencepost-problem

BALTIMORE COUNTY PUBLIC SCHOOLS. "Money Activities on a Hundred Chart."
bcps.org/parents/pdf/Money-Activities-on-a-Hundred-Chart.pdf (PDF)

BEARDSLEY, LEAH MILDRED. *1001 Uses of the Hundred Square: Activities and Ideas for Teaching Mathematics*, Parker Publishing Company, 1973.
archive.org/details/1001UsesOfTheHundredSquares-LeahMildredBeardsley

BOGOMOLNY, ALEXANDER. "Euclid's Game," Cut the Knot Interactive Mathematics Miscellany and Puzzles website.
cut-the-knot.org/blue/EuclidAlg.shtml

BOOLE, MARY EVEREST. *The preparation of the child for science,* The Clarendon Press, 1904. Available at the Internet Archive.
archive.org/details/preparationofchi00boolrich

BOSCHEN, JESSICA. "A Twist on the 100's Chart," What I Have Learned Teaching blog, August 29, 2013.
whatihavelearnedteaching.com/0-99-chart-freebie

BOUCHER, DONNA. "Humpty Dumpty 120 Chart ... Putting the Pieces

Together Again," Math Coach's Corner blog, October 2014.
mathcoachscorner.com/2014/10/
    humpty-dumpty-120-chart-putting-the-pieces-together-again

BURNS, MARILYN. "Can ⅓ + ⅓ = ⅖? It seemed so!" Marilyn Burns Math Blog, March 22, 2018.
marilynburnsmathblog.com/can-1-3-1-3-2-6-it-seemed-so

BUSCAGLIA, LEO F. "It is paradoxical …" Frequently quoted in print and online, but unsourced.
en.wikiquote.org/wiki/Talk:Leo_Buscaglia

CAPES, RACHEL. "Grab a Free Adding and Subtracting Movement Game—Wiggle to 100," You've Got This Math blog, January 19, 2016.
youvegotthismath.com/2016/01/19/wiggle-to-100

—. "Here's a Free Number Puzzle Game to Develop Number Sense," You've Got This Math blog, July 27, 2016.
youvegotthismath.com/2016/07/27/numberpuzzlegame

CLEMENTS, DOUG. "You know what? Children like mathematics …" from "Why Early Childhood is the Right Time to Start Learning Math," McGraw-Hill Education PreK-12 on YouTube, November 22, 2013.
youtu.be/B2Z0djuCDKA

COKER, LACY. "Cultivating thinking skills …" from "5 Tips to Cultivate Math Curiosity," Play Discover Learn blog, December 28, 2017. If you're teaching young children, be sure to check out her free twelve-week Early Math Discovery Course.
playdiscoverlearn247.com/2017/12/28/5-tips-to-cultivate-math-curiosity
playdiscoverlearn247.com/members/guided-discovery-course

DANIELSON, CHRISTOPHER. "The sequence machine," Overthinking My Teaching blog, March 11, 2016.
christopherdanielson.wordpress.com/2016/03/11/the-sequence-machine

DARGAUD, GUILLAUME & JENNIFER. "How to prove that all odd numbers are prime," personal website.
gdargaud.net/Humor/OddPrime.html

DEVLIN, KEITH. "At heart, mathematical thinking is …" from "How today's pros solve math problems: Part 3 (The Nueva School course)," Devlin's Angle blog, April 4, 2018.
devlinsangle.blogspot.com/2018/04/how-todays-pros-solve-math-problems.html

FETTER, ANNIE. "Ever Wonder What They'd Notice?" The Math Forum at NCTM, YouTube video, June 8, 2015.
youtu.be/a-Fth6sOaRA

FINKEL, DAN. "The Hundred Chart Game," Math for Love blog, January 1, 2016.
mathforlove.com/lesson/the-hundred-chart-game

FLETCHER, GRAHAM. "Bottoms Up to Conceptually Understanding Numbers," GFletchy blog, October 10, 2014.
gfletchy.com/2014/10/10/bottoms-up-to-conceptually-understanding-numbers

GASKINS, DENISE. "You don't need a set of worksheets …" from "Playing Complex Fractions with Your Kids," Let's Play Math blog, October 23, 2018.
denisegaskins.com/2018/10/22/playing-complex-fractions-with-your-kids

——. *Hundred Charts Galore!* printables file.
tabletopacademy.net/free-printables

——. "Tens Concentration," Let's Play Math blog, July 10, 2007.
denisegaskins.com/2007/07/10/tens-concentration

——. "Math Club Nim," Let's Play Math blog, July 19, 2007.
denisegaskins.com/2007/07/19/math-club-nim

——. "Math with Many Right Answers," Let's Play Math blog, August 3, 2015.
denisegaskins.com/2015/08/03/math-with-many-right-answers

——. "Mathematics Is Worthy," Let's Play Math blog, August 15, 2018.
denisegaskins.com/2018/08/15/mathematics-is-worthy

GROSS, HERB. "What's really neat …" from a lecture on problem solving.
mathasasecondlanguage.org

HAMILTON, GORDON AND LORA SAARNIO. "Blotch," MathPickle website, 2018.
mathpickle.com/project/blotch

HOLLOWELL, MALIA. "Ask a first grader what number comes after 100 …" from "15 Brilliant Ways to Use a Hundred Chart," The STEM Laboratory blog, January 19, 2016.
thestemlaboratory.com/15-brilliant-ways-use-hundred-chart

HUDSON, LEAH. "Preschool Math Game w/Free Printable," Simple Home Blessing blog, 2016.
simplehomeblessing.com/preschool-math-game

KAEHLER, LORIE KING. "Post-it Sticky Notes Hundred Chart," Reading Confetti blog, January 2015.
readingconfetti.com/2015/01/post-it-sticky-notes-hundred-chart.html

KAWAS, TERRY. "Hundred Board Logic," MathWire website, 1994.
mathwire.com/problemsolving/hblogic.pdf (PDF)

—. "Guess the Number," MathWire website, 2004.
mathwire.com/problemsolving/guessthenumber.pdf (PDF)

KAY, STUART. "Blank 100 Grid Number Investigations," TES website, November 13, 2017. Free registration required for download.
tes.com/teaching-resource/blank-100-grid-number-investigations-6340939

KAYE, PEGGY. "Games teach or reinforce many of the skills …" from *Games for Math,* Pantheon, 1988. If you're homeschooling young children, be sure to check out the other books in Kaye's *Games for…* series.
peggykaye.com

KRANENBURG, JENN. Quoted by Malke Rosenfeld in "Moving Scale Math on the Hundred Chart," Math on the Move blog, October 5, 2016.
mathonthemovebook.com/2016/10/05/moving-scale-math-on-the-hundred-chart

LAWLER, MIKE. "An introduction to random walks for kids," Mike's Math Page blog, June 19, 2016.
mikesmathpage.wordpress.com/2016/06/19/an-introduction-to-random-walks-for-kids

—. "Random walks with kids," Mike's Math Page blog, April 8, 2017.
mikesmathpage.wordpress.com/2017/04/08/random-walks-with-kids

LEO, LUCINDA. "My long-term goal …" from "3 Things I've Learned About Homeschooling in 2013," Navigating by Joy blog, December 10, 2013.
navigatingbyjoy.com/2013/12/10/3-things-ive-learned-homeschooling-2013

LOMBARD, BILL AND BRAD FULTON. "The Tax Collector," *Simply Great Math Activities,* Teacher to Teacher Press. Mr. L's Math blog archive.
tinyurl.com/taxcollectorgame (PDF)

MASCOTT, AMY. "Action Action 1, 2, 3 Get Kids Moving, Writing, Thinking," Teach Mama blog, 2009.
teachmama.com/action-action-1-2-3

MATH FORUM TEAM. "Beginning to Problem Solve with I Notice/I Wonder" The Math Forum archive, 2011.
tinyurl.com/brainstorm-math (PDF)

McManaman, Yelena. "The Hundred Chart," Natural Math blog, December 13, 2012.
naturalmath.com/2012/12/the-hundred-chart

—. "The Hundred Chart and Game Cards," Natural Math blog, January 16, 2013.
MoebiusNoodles.com/2013/01/The-Hundred-Chart-And-Game-Cards

Nrich Team. "Next-door Numbers," Nrich Enriching Mathematics website.
nrich.maths.org/13665

—. "Charlie's Delightful Machine," Nrich Enriching Mathematics website.
nrich.maths.org/7024

—. "Factors and Multiples Game," Nrich Enriching Mathematics website.
nrich.maths.org/5468
nrich.maths.org/5468/solution

Ohanian, Susan. "Mathematics is a process of constructing knowledge ..." from *Garbage Pizza, Patchwork Quilts, and Math Magic: Stories about Teachers who Love to Teach and Children who Love to Learn*, W. H. Freeman, 1992.

Orr, Jon. "Pentomino Puzzles," Mr. Orr Is a Geek blog, September 30, 2016.
mrorr-isageek.com/pentomino-puzzles

Parker, Ruth. "I used to think my job was to teach students ..." from "The Having of Mathematical Ideas: Learning to Listen to Students," presentation at NCSM Annual Conference, 2013.

Pantozzi, Ralph. "Random Walk," National Museum of Mathematics, The 2014 Rosenthal Prize for Innovation in Math Teaching.
momath.org/wp-content/uploads/2016/11/Random-Walk-lesson-9.12.15.pdf (PDF)

Pfeiffer, Sherron. *Creating NIM Games,* Math Project Series, Dale Seymour, 1998.

Randolph, Winifred and Verne G. Jeffers. "A new look for the hundreds chart," *The Arithmetic Teacher,* Vol. 21, No. 3, March 1974.
jstor.org/stable/41188490

Ray-Riek, Max. "Everyone can notice something ..." from *Powerful Problem Solving: Activities for Sense Making with the Mathematical Practices,* Heinemann Publishing, 2013.

——. "Noticing and Wondering in High School," The Max Ray Blog, August 28, 2013.
tinyurl.com/maxray-noticing

ROSENFELD, MALKE. "Allowing students' bodies to interact …" from "Getting Started with Whole-Body Math Learning: Scale Up!" Math on the Move blog, February 19, 2017.
mathonthemovebook.com/2017/02/19/
    getting-started-with-whole-body-math-learning-scale-up

——. "We want math to make sense …" from *Math on the Move: Engaging Students in Whole Body Learning,* Heinemann Publishing, 2016.

SALLAY, IVA. Find the Factors blog.
findthefactors.com

SCAPTURA, CHRISTOPHER, JENNIFER SUH, AND GREG MAHAFFEY. "Masterpieces to Mathematics: Using Art to Teach Fraction, Decimal, and Percent Equivalents," *Mathematics Teaching in the Middle School,* vol. 13, no. 1, August 2007.
nctm.org/Publications/mathematics-teaching-in-middle-school/2007/Vol13/Issue1/
    mtms2007-08-24a_pdf (PDF)

SCHMIDT, MEGAN. "Spiraling Math on a Stick," Number Loving Beagle blog, August 26, 2016.
mathybeagle.com/2016/08/26/spiraling-math-on-a-stick

——. "Spiraling the Hundred Chart and Beyond," Number Loving Beagle blog, December 12, 2017.
mathybeagle.com/2017/12/12/spiraling-the-hundred-chart-and-beyond

——. "Holy Hundreds Chart!" Number Loving Beagle blog, March 30, 2018.
mathybeagle.com/2018/03/30/holy-hundreds-chart

SCHWARTZ, JOE. "Number Grids and Number Lines: Can They Live Together in Peace?" Exit 10A blog, November 13, 2014.
exit10a.blogspot.com/2014/11/number-grids-and-number-lines-can-they.html

——. "I Like This Game Because You Have to Think Hard," Exit 10A blog, January 6, 2016.
exit10a.blogspot.com/2016/01/i-like-this-game-because-you-have-to.html

SHASHIN, VLADIMIR. "Gomoku," PC Gaming website, 1999.
pcgaming.ws/viewgame.php?game=gomoku

SHEAKOSKI, MEGAN. "Sticky Hundreds Chart Math Activity." Coffee Cups and Crayons blog, January 22, 2014
coffeecupsandcrayons.com/sticky-hundreds-chart-math-activity

SHORE, CHRIS. Clothesline Math website.
clotheslinemath.com

SOROOSHIAN, PAM. "Games and Math," Sandra Dodd's Unschoolers and Mathematics website.
sandradodd.com/math/pamgames

STADEL, ANDREW. Estimation 180 website, including his "Clothesline Math" page.
estimation180.com/days.html
estimation180.com/clothesline.html

STEEN, LYNN ARTHUR. "What humans do with the language of mathematics ..." from "Pattern," *On the Shoulders of Giants: New Approaches to Numeracy,* The National Academies Press, 1990.
nap.edu/catalog/1532/on-the-shoulders-of-giants-new-approaches-to-numeracy

STEIN, ULAM AND WELLS. "A visual display of some properties of the distribution of primes", *American Mathematics Monthly,* vol. 71, no. 5, May 1964.

STEVENS, JOHN. Would You Rather? website.
wouldyourathermath.com

STOHR-HUNT, PATRICIA. "Instructional Conundrum: 100 Board or 0–99 Chart?," Bookish Ways in Math and Science blog, October 23, 2013.
bookishways.blogspot.com/2013/10/instructional-conundrum-100-board-or-0.html

THOMPSON, TERRI. "Driveway Hundred Chart Game," Creative Family Fun blog, 2015.
creativefamilyfun.net/driveway-hundred-char

TRUCHET, SEBASTIEN. "Mémoire sur les combinaisons," from *Histoire de l'Academie royale des sciences, De l'imprimerie royale,* 1745. Available at Google Books.
books.google.com/books?id=NgkVAAAAQAAJ

VUORINEN, AAPELI AND YONI NAZARATHY. "Who Gets to be on the Multiplication Table?" One on Epsilon blog, February 2, 2018.
oneonepsilon.com/single-post/2018/01/28/
How-Many-Times-Does-a-Number-Appear-on-the-Times-Table

WARREN, BECKY. "Pattern Maker," Lines Curves Spirals blog, February 8, 2018.
linescurvesspirals.blogspot.co.uk/2018/02/diy-pattern-maker.html

WEISSTEIN, ERIC W. "196-Algorithm." from MathWorld—A Wolfram Web Resource.
mathworld.wolfram.com/196-Algorithm.html

WIKIPEDIA CONTRIBUTORS. "Bézier curve," Wikipedia Internet Encyclopedia.
en.wikipedia.org/wiki/B%C3%A9zier_curve

——. "Lychrel number," Wikipedia Internet Encyclopedia.
en.wikipedia.org/wiki/Lychrel_number

——. "Nim," Wikipedia Internet Encyclopedia.
en.wikipedia.org/wiki/Nim

——. "Off-by-one error," Wikipedia Internet Encyclopedia.
en.wikipedia.org/wiki/Off-by-one_error

——. "Op Art," Wikipedia Internet Encyclopedia.
en.wikipedia.org/wiki/Op_art

——. "Pentomino," Wikipedia Internet Encyclopedia.
en.wikipedia.org/wiki/Pentomino

——. "Random walk," Wikipedia Internet Encyclopedia.
en.wikipedia.org/wiki/Random_walk

——. "Truchet tiles," Wikipedia Internet Encyclopedia.
en.wikipedia.org/wiki/Truchet_tiles

——. "Ulam Spiral," Wikipedia Internet Encyclopedia.
en.wikipedia.org/wiki/Ulam_spiral

——. "Zhoubi Suanjing," Wikipedia Internet Encyclopedia.
en.wikipedia.org/wiki/Zhoubi_Suanjing

YOUCUBED TEAM. "How Close to 100?" YouCubed at Stanford University website.
youcubed.org/tasks/how-close-to-100

ZASLAVSKY, CLAUDIA. "Language should be part of the activity …" from *Preparing Young Children for Mathematics: A Book of Games with Updated Book, Game and Resource Lists,* Schocken Books, 1986.

About
the Author

DENISE GASKINS ENJOYS MATH, AND she delights in sharing that joy with young people. "Math is not just rules and rote memory," she says. "Math is like ice cream, with more flavors than you can imagine. And if all you ever do is textbook math, that's like eating broccoli-flavored ice cream."

A veteran homeschooling mother of five, Denise has taught or tutored mathematics at every level from pre-K to undergraduate physics "which," she explains, "at least in the recitation class I taught, was just one story problem after another. What fun!"

Now she writes the popular Let's Play Math blog and manages the monthly Playful Math Education blog carnival.

A Note from Denise

I hope you enjoyed this book and found new ideas that will help your children enjoy learning. I'd love to connect with you online and to hear your family's experiences with mathematical play.

If you believe this book is worth sharing, please consider posting a review on Goodreads, LibraryThing, or your favorite bookseller's website. An honest review is the highest compliment you can pay to any author, and your comments help fellow readers discover good books.

Thank you!

— DENISE GASKINS

LET'S CONNECT ONLINE: DeniseGaskins.com, LetsPlayMath@gmail.com

Books by Denise Gaskins

tabletopacademy.net/playful-math-books

"Denise has gathered up a treasure trove of living math resources for busy parents. If you've ever struggled to see how to make math come alive beyond your math curriculum (or if you've ever considered teaching math without a curriculum), you'll want to check out this book."
— KATE SNOW, AUTHOR OF *MULTIPLICATION FACTS THAT STICK*

Let's Play Math:

How Families Can Learn Math

Together — and Enjoy It

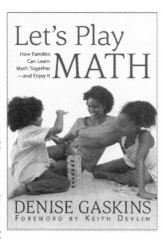

Transform your child's experience of math!

Even if you struggled with mathematics in school, you can help your children enjoy learning and prepare them for academic success.

Author Denise Gaskins makes it easy with this mixture of math games, low-prep project ideas, and inspiring coffee-chat advice from a veteran homeschooling mother of five. Drawing on more than thirty years' teaching experience, Gaskins provides helpful tips for parents with kids from preschool to high school, whether your children learn at home or attend a traditional classroom.

Don't let your children suffer from the epidemic of math anxiety. Pick up a copy of *Let's Play Math*, and start enjoying math today.

Want to help your kids learn math? Claim your free copy of Denise's 24-page problem-solving booklet, and sign up to hear about new books, revisions, and sales or other promotions.

TabletopAcademy.net/Subscribe

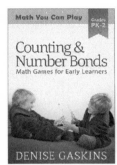
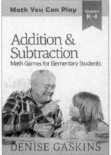

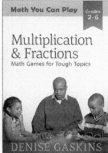

The *Math You Can Play* Series

You'll love these math games because they give your child a strong foundation for mathematical success.

By playing these games, you strengthen your child's intuitive understanding of numbers and build problem-solving strategies. Mastering a math game can be hard work. But kids do it willingly because it's fun.

Math games prevent math anxiety. Games pump up your child's mental muscles, reduce the fear of failure, and generate a positive attitude toward mathematics.

So what are you waiting for? Clear off a table, grab a deck of cards, and let's play some math.

Under Construction: The *Playful Math Singles* Series

The Playful Math Singles from Tabletop Academy Press are short, topical books featuring clear explanations and ready-to-play activities.

Word Problems from Literature features story problems for elementary and middle school students based on family-favorite books such as *Mr. Popper's Penguins* and *The Hobbit*. Step by step solutions demonstrate how bar model diagrams can help children reason their way to the answer.

70+ Things To Do with a Hundred Chart shows you how to take your child on a mathematical adventure through playful, practical activities. Who knew math could be so much fun?

More titles coming soon. Watch for them at your favorite online bookstore.

Made in the USA
Columbia, SC
15 September 2020

20775621R00083